Sweet Gratitude

Sweet Gratitude

bake a thank-you
for the really important
people in your life

Judith Sutton

ARTISAN

New York

Also by Judith Sutton

Champagne & Caviar & Other Delicacies
Truffles: Ultimate Luxury, Everyday Pleasure
(with Rosario Safina)

Published by Artisan
A Division of Workman Publishing, Inc.
708 Broadway
New York, New York 10003-9555
www.artisanbooks.com

Library of Congress Cataloging-in-Publication Data
Sutton, Judith C., 1949–
Sweet gratitude : bake a thank-you for the really important people in your life /
Judith Sutton
p. cm.
ISBN-10: 1-57965-261-1
ISBN-13: 987-157965-2616
1. Desserts. 2. Baking. I. Title
TX773.S976 2005
641.8'6—dc22   2004062264

Printed in Singapore
10 9 8 7 6 5 4 3 2 1

Book design by Vivian Ghazarian

To the Cat Doctor

CONTENTS

INTRODUCTION

This book really started at my vet's office. A couple of years ago, my cat, Remy, had to see
an oncologist regularly. Because at the time I happened to be baking a lot of cookies (actually,
about a hundred and fifty dozen or so) for another cookbook project, I started taking some
of them along for Dr. Rocha (aka "the Cat Doctor") and his staff each time we visited them.
By the time I finished the cookie project, Remy was doing so well that I had started referring
to her as Dr. Rocha's poster child—and I was so grateful that I went on baking special treats
for them whenever she had an appointment. When I told a friend about the excitement—perhaps
pandemonium would be a better word—the Caramel-Topped Turtle Brownies caused one day,
this book was born.

      I've always baked for the important people in my life, starting with the birthday cake
I made for my mother when I was ten (from a mix, of course). I've baked many birthday
cakes for family and friends since then, and I've baked a lot of thank-yous, for everyone from
the neighbor who helped on moving day to a friend who babysat for Remy to my eye doctor
after he'd opened his office at ten o'clock on a Saturday night to see me (everything turned
out fine). My friends who live in other cities are always amazed at my stories about how New
York is really just a small town, but it's true. My courtly UPS man is so happy when he can
deliver something fun like chocolates rather than the boxes of editing projects he usually brings
me that I share some of my favorite cookies with him. The guys at the Mail Boxes store are so
helpful—and so fascinated—when I need color copies of some of my dessert articles that I bake
them something too. And then there is my Christmas tree seller (each year, college students
like Andrina come down from Canada and set up a mini tree stand at the end of my street).
After I'd bought my tree one especially cold winter, I stopped by with a tin of little sweets. The
next year Andrina greeted me as "the Cookie Lady"—and now she reserves an especially
beautiful tree for me.

A home-baked treat from someone's kitchen is always special: No matter how simple, it shows that you care enough to have taken the time to make it. (In fact, when time is at a premium, you can seek out one of the many recipes that can be made in a matter of minutes. Just look for the clock symbol ⏱ before the recipe's title.) Whether they take a few minutes or more than a few, however, homemade sweets can be a comfort or a celebration or both. I've made my favorite brownies for a friend's surprise birthday party, and I've baked them for another friend who was in mourning. The act of baking can be a solace as well, when you are in need of comfort yourself—especially when the recipes are as easy as those in this book.

Many of these recipes, such as the five-minute Brown Sugar Shortbread or the Spicy English Gingersnaps, are simple enough for even the most inexperienced baker. While some of them are homey—Old-fashioned Spice Cake with Cream Cheese Frosting—and others are more sophisticated—Super-Easy Lemon Tart or Chocolate Espresso Sandwich Cookies— none of them is difficult.

Because these treats are intended for giving, all of them can be made entirely ahead, often several days in advance—or even earlier, since most of the cookies and brownies, for example, can be frozen for several weeks. As simple as they are, some can also be prepared in stages, so you'll find advance preparation notes, as well as keeping and storage information. In some cases, I've included suggestions for last-minute garnishes or serving ideas for when you might be taking them to a potluck supper or a friend's dinner party. They are also just the thing for entertaining at home or for special occasions with your own family (they are certainly among the most important people in your life). And don't forget to treat yourself. The cookie and bar recipes make enough so that you can keep some for your own special stash; even the tartlet recipes each make four individual tarts—two or three to give away, one or two to keep if you like.

Many of these recipes include variations that sometimes turn them into entirely different desserts. The batter for the Devil's Food Cupcakes, for example, baked in round pans, makes a wonderful birthday cake. And for chocolate lovers, the Peanut Butter Cookies with

Crunch can easily be "chocolate-chipped," and you can speckle the Coconut Macaroons with chopped chocolate. Look for the shortcut versions of recipes that do take a little more time: Both the Coconut Layer Cake and Old-fashioned Spice Cake offer easy sheet cake variations, and when you don't have the time for rolled and cut-out cookies for the holidays, make the slice-and-bake version of the Brown Sugar Cookies.

Of course, all of these are year-round treats, but there are many that are perfect for the holidays: Those brown sugar cookies and the Ginger-Ginger Petticoat Tails are just two of the cookies that are naturals at Christmastime (you can bake them ahead, before things get really hectic, and freeze them, all ready to go). Woo your valentine with Raspberry Linzer Hearts or top the Blueberry-Raspberry Tart with whipped cream for a red-white-and-blue Fourth of July. And the cupcake duo, devil's food and orange, will delight the scariest goblin on Halloween.

Whether for a care package to your homesick college student, the holiday tins you make for the sweet-lovers on your list, or just something special you suddenly decide to send to a dear friend, many of these confections also ship well. Most of the cookies and bars are good choices, as well as the Candied Orange Peel and Totally Unlike Store-Bought Caramels; even some of the cakes or cakelets are good travelers (see page 19 for tips on packing your baked goods for shipping).

All of these recipes have been tested and retested in my home kitchen, and they've also been taste tested by friends and other demanding dessert lovers. When I started working on the book, I realized that I had a ready-and-eager tasting panel at my vet's office (conveniently located a block from my apartment). But this time I made them do a little work for their treats: I had them fill out tasting sheets each time I brought them something.

I hope that you enjoy baking and giving these desserts as much as I did—and that these recipes will sweeten your bonds with the important people in your life.

Chocolate and Cocoa Powder

For unsweetened chocolate, a brand such as Ghirardelli, found in the baking aisle of many supermarkets, will give your brownies a noticeably better flavor than ordinary supermarket unsweetened chocolate. Bittersweet and semisweet chocolate can usually be used interchangeably in recipes, depending on your personal preference; I usually use bittersweet because I like a deeper chocolate flavor. Callebaut is an excellent Belgian chocolate available in many gourmet markets; or look for brands such as Lindt and Tobler (these usually come in 3½-ounce bars) in the candy aisle of the supermarket. For milk chocolate, choose one of these three brands or Ghirardelli. When you want white chocolate (which isn't really chocolate at all, since it doesn't contain any cocoa liquor, the pure ground cacao bean paste that is the basis for all chocolates), read the label carefully and be sure to buy a brand that contains cocoa butter—some white chocolate is made with vegetable fat and doesn't contain any of the cacao bean at all.

Nestlé, of course, makes the classic chocolate chips (regular, minis, chunks, etc.), but Ghirardelli and other manufacturers are now producing a variety of chunks and chips, big and little. For most recipes, however, I like to use high-quality chocolate and cut or chop it into chunks, shards, or morsels rather than using manufactured chocolate chips, which are made with artificial vanilla and just don't have the more intense flavor of better chocolates. (Note that chocolate chips are formulated to keep their shape during baking and do not melt well—so they should not be substituted for other types of chocolate.) It's usually easier to cut up one of the 3½-ounce bars, which make nice shards, than a big slab of chocolate.

There are two types of unsweetened cocoa powder: natural, or nonalkalized, and Dutch-process, or alkalized. Dutched cocoa has been treated to make it less acidic than natural cocoa powder and it has a richer, deeper color, but it actually has less flavor than high-quality nonalkalized cocoa. The two types can't always be used interchangeably in a recipe because they can react differently with baking powder or baking soda, so check the label carefully when you are buying cocoa for a recipe that calls for one or the other (Droste and Hershey's European-style are the most widely available alkalized cocoa powders; Hershey's regular is a good natural cocoa). However, when neither type is specified in these recipes, you can use either one.

To chop chocolate into shards, use a sharp heavy knife. It's easiest to cut thin 3½-ounce bars (such as Lindt) into free-form shards, and those are what I usually use: First cut the bars crosswise into roughly ¼-inch-wide strips, or the width specified in the recipe (it doesn't matter if these break as you cut, which they will—and you will probably end up with some chocolate shavings as well), then cut across the strips on the diagonal to make ½- to ¾-inch-long pieces, or as specified. Precision is not the goal here: The pieces will vary in size, and that is just fine. To cut a thicker bar or slab of chocolate into shards, cut it into roughly ¼-inch-wide pieces, then lay these pieces on their side and cut lengthwise into narrower widths as necessary; finally, cut across the strips into smaller pieces as above.

To make chocolate shavings or curls, use a vegetable peeler and a thick slab or chunk of chocolate (I have made these using 1-ounce squares of semisweet chocolate, but a thicker piece is easier to work with and the results are better). The chocolate should be at warm room temperature; if necessary, put it on a plate under a table lamp for a few minutes to warm it up, or put it in the microwave for no more than 10 seconds. The heat of your hands will also warm the chocolate as you work; hold the chocolate in a piece of plastic wrap if you don't want to end up with melted chocolate on your hands, and turn the piece of chocolate occasionally so the part you are holding doesn't begin to melt.

For shavings—to mound on a pie, for example—run the peeler in quick strokes over the chocolate. You can shave the chocolate directly onto a dessert or let the shavings drop onto a sheet of waxed paper and then shake them from the paper onto the dessert. For curls, run the peeler more slowly along the chocolate, pressing lightly for thinner curls, more firmly for thicker curls (if the curls break into shavings, the chocolate is too cold and should be briefly warmed again). If you dropped the curls onto a sheet of waxed paper, use a paring knife or a toothpick to transfer the curls to the top of your dessert—they are delicate, and if you use your hands to move them, they may melt.

Chocolate math: Results may vary slightly, depending on how finely or coarsely the chocolate is chopped, but 4 ounces of chocolate will make about 1 scant cup of chocolate shards or coarsely chopped chocolate, or about ¾ cup of finely chopped chocolate.

Butter

Unsalted butter tends to be fresher than salted—the salt can mask off-flavors, and salted butter may be allowed to sit on the shelf longer than unsalted. More to the point for baking, unsalted butter allows you to control the amount of salt in the recipe, adding a precise amount (there's no way to tell how much salt a salted butter contains). Some people are surprised to learn that many, if not most, desserts include salt in the ingredients lists (in making these recipes, I used ordinary table salt). Salt helps bring out flavors, and a piecrust or cookie made without any salt can taste "flat." Butter is a handy freezer staple; wrap it well so it doesn't pick up other flavors.

Cream

Depending on its producer, cream (other than light or coffee cream) may be labeled "heavy cream," "heavy whipping cream," or "whipping cream." Heavy and heavy whipping cream both contain 36 to 40 percent butterfat; whipping cream has 30 to 36 percent. I prefer the richer heavy cream. Despite its name, whipping cream, because of its lower butterfat content, does not whip as easily as heavy cream, and once whipped, it is less stable. If possible, buy pasteurized rather than ultrapasteurized cream, though pasteurized cream is increasingly difficult to find. Ultrapasteurized cream has been treated to extend its shelf life, and the process gives it a slight off-flavor; it also doesn't whip as well.

To whip cream, always start with very cold cream. Especially on a hot day, or if your kitchen is hot, it's helpful to chill the bowl and beaters in the freezer or refrigerator. An electric mixer is fast and easy, but for small amounts, I sometimes use an old-fashioned rotary beater.

Keep in mind that cream will whip to twice its volume, so choose a bowl that's large enough, preferably a deep one. Start beating on low speed, to avoid splatters; once the cream has started to thicken, you can increase the speed. For soft peaks, beat until the cream just holds slightly droopy peaks when the beaters are lifted. For stiff peaks, beat until the cream just holds firm peaks that keep their shape when the beaters are lifted. In either case, be careful not to overwhip the cream—when using an electric mixer, I reduce the speed to low when the cream is almost to the stage I want and finish beating it on that speed.

Buttermilk

Although buttermilk was originally the liquid that remained after butter was churned from cream, these days commercial buttermilk is produced by adding a bacterial culture to low-fat or nonfat milk. Either low-fat or nonfat buttermilk is fine for the recipes in this book. Powdered dry buttermilk is also available, found with the other baking ingredients in many supermarkets. It has a long shelf life, which means that you can use just what you need for one recipe, then store the rest for later.

Eggs

Use large eggs for these recipes (white or brown—the color of the shell is related to the type of hen and has nothing to do with the flavor or quality of the egg inside).

It's easiest to separate eggs when they are cold, so if a recipe calls for whites and/or yolks, separate the eggs right after taking them out of the refrigerator. Most cookbooks tell you to bring egg whites to room temperature before beating them for a meringue, the prevailing belief being that they will whip to a greater volume. You can leave them at room temperature for thirty minutes or set the bowl of whites in a larger bowl of hot water to warm them, but in most cases the difference is really minimal—I don't worry about it unless I'm making something like angel food cake.

When I'm adding the eggs to a cake batter or cookie dough, I always break each one into a cup first (usually the measuring cup I just used for the flour or sugar) before pouring it into the mixing bowl. That way, I avoid adding a "bad" egg (a highly unlikely possibility these days) or any bits of shell (more likely) to the batter or dough.

To beat egg whites, always start with a clean, dry bowl and beaters; even a trace of grease (or a speck of yolk) can prevent the whites from rising to their full volume, so it's also important to be careful when separating eggs. Beat on medium speed until the whites are foamy (if there is salt and/or cream of tartar in the recipe, it is usually added to the whites at this point). Increase the speed to medium-high to high and beat until the whites reach the desired stage. For soft peaks (the stage at which you add the sugar if making a meringue), beat until the whites hold slightly droopy peaks when the beaters are lifted. For stiff peaks, beat until the whites hold firm upright peaks when the beaters are lifted; the whites should still be shiny, not dry—overbeaten whites can become clumpy and are difficult to incorporate into a mousse base or batter. For meringue, add the sugar gradually as you beat the whites to firm, glossy peaks; because of the sugar, the peaks will not be quite as firm as egg whites beaten without sugar.

Sugars

A few of these recipes use superfine sugar, which dissolves more quickly than regular granulated. Sometimes referred to as bar sugar, it's available in most supermarkets, but if you don't have superfine on hand, you can easily make your own by processing granulated sugar in a food processor until fine.

With brown sugars, dark brown has more molasses added than light brown, and it imparts a deeper taste of caramel. Flavor aside, light and dark brown sugar can be used interchangeably in most recipes, depending on your preference; if light or dark is not specified in these recipes, either one is fine.

Vanilla and Other Extracts

Always use pure vanilla and other extracts: Artificial vanilla extract, not surprisingly, tastes artificial. Vanilla beans impart the truest and most intense vanilla flavor—if they are fresh and not dried out, that is—and you'll love the taste that just a half bean adds to the filling for Apple and Brown Butter Crostata, for example. Vanilla beans are perishable, and their flavor diminishes over time, but they keep exceptionally well, tightly wrapped, in the freezer.

Lemons and Other Citrus Fruit

The zest of a citrus fruit, such as an orange or lemon, is the colored portion of the peel, without any of the bitter white pith. Before the advent of the Microplane, a handy gadget to own, grating lemon or other zest on a box grater was a tedious affair, invariably resulting in grated knuckles as well. The Microplane is a rasp-type grater with a long "blade" set into a plastic handle (there are now several versions, but the original cheese grater–zester is very versatile), and it really makes zesting citrus fruit a breeze. You can hold the grater in one hand and run the fruit down it with the other, as with a traditional box grater, but my friend Lori ("the Lemon Queen") advises stroking the grater across the fruit "as if you were playing a violin." The Microplane makes light, fluffy shavings, so be sure to pack the shavings into the measuring spoon for an accurate measure.

NOTES ON STORING, SHIPPING, AND WRAPPING

To keep the cookies, cakes, and other sweets you've made at their best, you want to treat them well. Many can be made in advance and stored for several days or more; some can be frozen. And whether you are mailing cookies across the country or just delivering a cake to a neighbor across the street, you want it to make a great impression. Here is all the information you need, including creative ideas for packaging your home-baked thank-yous.

Storing and Freezing

The individual recipes provide specific keeping and storing information where appropriate, but there are certain basic guidelines to keep in mind. Most cookies keep well at room temperature for at least five days. Sturdy tins are still the best way to store all cookies, as well as most brownies and bars (and even some little cakes). Plastic storage containers with tight-fitting lids are another option—the reusable/disposable ones are handy, especially if you have baked a variety of different types of cookies. And heavy-duty plastic storage bags work for sturdier cookies and bars. Be sure to store crisp cookies and soft cookies separately—if they are packed together, crisp ones will soften and soft ones will dry out.

Although plain cakes and some pies and tarts can simply be wrapped or covered with plastic wrap, cake keepers are useful for both storing and transporting cakes, and pies and tarts too. But if you don't have a cake keeper, you can use an inverted large bowl to cover a frosted cake on the counter. Or drape a sheet of plastic wrap loosely over the top, using a few strategically placed toothpicks to keep the wrap from touching the frosting. This is also a good way to cover a whipped-cream pie or other refrigerated dessert without marring the surface of the filling or topping. Or use a foil tent when you want to cover a dessert without disturbing its surface: Tent a large sheet of foil loosely over the pie or tart and carefully crimp it against the edge of the pie plate in a few places or slip the edges of the foil under the tart pan.

Most cookies and brownies can be frozen for at least two weeks. Filled cookies generally do not freeze well, nor do frosted cookies (but you can freeze plain unfrosted cookies to be decorated later). Many cookies, such as chocolate chips and gingersnaps, can simply be stored in heavy-duty freezer bags (I like to double-bag them); squeeze the air out of the bags before sealing them. Cut-out cookies and other more fragile ones should be layered between sheets of waxed paper in an airtight freezer container; if they do not fill the container, protect them with some crumpled waxed paper. Wrap brownies and bars—individually or in small groups or stacks—tightly in plastic wrap, then wrap them in aluminum foil or put them in plastic freezer bags.

Be sure to label the packages or containers of whatever you freeze! And defrost the cookies and bars (or other frozen baked goods) still wrapped, so any condensation that forms will be on the packaging, not on the surface of the baked good.

Many cookie doughs can be made ahead and frozen for at least two weeks. This can be a timesaver during the holiday season, and it's always nice to have frozen dough waiting in the freezer: Make a double recipe the next time you are baking and freeze half the dough for later—or just bake a dozen or so from the basic recipe and freeze the rest. Wrap the dough tightly in plastic wrap and then in foil, and defrost it, still wrapped, in the refrigerator. Pie and tart doughs can be frozen and thawed in the same manner.

Shipping

To make sure your shipped cookies or brownies arrive intact rather than in crumbs, it's essential to cushion them well for their journey. Tins or other sturdy containers such as attractive cardboard or plastic boxes are essential. Layer the cookies or bars in the container between sheets of waxed paper and pack them tightly—you don't want them to shift or bump into each other. Mix and match cookies if you want, but remember to package crisp and soft cookies in separate containers. You might want to wrap brownies and other bars individually in plastic wrap before you pack them; you can also wrap pairs of cookies together, bottoms facing each other, in plastic wrap or foil for added security. Add a layer of crumpled waxed paper or colorful tissue paper to the top before you seal the container. The lid should fit tightly, but you can tape it shut too, for added freshness.

Small plain cakes—not frosted or glazed—also ship well. Wrap each one in plastic wrap and then foil, and pack one or two each in a tin or other rigid container. Confections such as caramels and candied citrus peel are sturdy enough that you could tuck in a colorful cellophane bag of them alongside a tin of cookies.

To protect your precious baked goods in transit, use a large sturdy box that will allow plenty of room for cushioning the container of sweets. Boxes and all sorts of packing materials are available at post offices, private mailing services, and office supply stores. Bubble wrap is a good choice, but crumpled newspaper works fine in most cases (and it's a lot cheaper); I use a combination. You might want to wrap the container itself in bubble wrap first. Then line the bottom of the box with a layer of packing material, put the container of goodies in the center of the box, and surround it on all sides with more packing material, finishing with a thick layer on top. Close the top of the box, but before sealing it, give it a gentle shake to make sure the container inside will not shift; add more bubble wrap and/or newspaper if necessary. Seal the box securely with strong mailing tape and check to make sure all the box seams (such as the one on the bottom) are tightly sealed as well. I usually cover the address label with clear shipping tape to protect it.

Send your packages first class or priority mail, or use one of the overnight (or two-day) shipping services. It's a good idea to send them early in the week so that they don't end up sitting in a warehouse over the weekend.

Wrapping Home-Baked Treats

A visit to any party shop will give you lots of ideas for packaging your home-baked treats, but you can have fun by thinking out of the box, as it were—now is the time to use your imagination.

Although you might start by collecting an assortment of cookie, cake, and tea tins, antique or not (yard sales are a great source), there are dozens of other possibilities. For example, in addition to tins and pretty boxes, party stores sell colored "take-out" containers in various sizes—perfect for cookies or confections. They also stock cellophane party bags, which can be filled with sweets and tied with shiny ribbons, as well as decorative miniature shopping bags. (The Internet can also be a great source. A simple search will lead you to online suppliers of decorative packaging of all sorts.)

You'll want a selection of brightly colored or patterned tissue paper to line whatever containers you choose. Tissue paper can also be used for wrapping cookies, bars, and little cakes—wrap them first in plastic wrap, of course. Colored cellophane, sold in rolls, also makes festive packaging—stack an assortment of cookies on a sturdy paper plate, wrap it all in a large square of cellophane, and tie it with ribbons in different colors.

Plain tins and ordinary cardboard boxes can be brightened with wrapping paper—wrap the lids and bottoms separately, so they are reusable. Or wrap them in colorful fabric and tie them with satin ribbons. Even brown paper lunch bags can be decorated with stickers or colored markers—a fun project for any kids you know. Or have the kids make their own gift boxes for teacher (or grandparent) thank-yous by painting or coloring designs on plain white boxes.

You can make the container itself part of your gift. Flea markets and yard sales are a good source for plates and platters of all sorts. Many gift shops sell inexpensive tin plates in various patterns, ready for a cake or some cookies. Pretty baskets in a wide variety of shapes and sizes can hold all sorts of baked goods or jars of sweet sauces. Line the baskets with cloth napkins or a decorative kitchen towel. Stop by a big container store for more inspiration— stylish drawer or desk organizers, for example, can serve as cookie carriers.

Baking equipment can also serve as packaging—bake a pie in a pretty ceramic pie plate bought just for the occasion. Or include a new kitchen utensil along with your baked treats— tie two or three of those heatproof spatulas or spoons in contrasting colors together with a raffia bow and slip them into a goodie bag. Package a handy Microplane grater along with a lemon dessert—when your friend requests the recipe to bake it herself, she'll be all ready to zest the lemons! Tie a fanciful cutter onto a bag filled with cookies or tuck several into the tin. Many kitchenware shops sell unusual cookie cutters, including boxed sets of whimsical small cutters.

Baking supply stores also stock a wide variety of cookie cutters, along with all sorts of decorating tools, including edible decorations not found in the supermarket. (Christmas tree and other festive sprinkles are fun to include in your holiday cookie tins.) These suppliers also offer a range of handy kitchen gadgets to delight any baker, as well as cardboard cake rounds— wrapped in foil or plastic, rounds are great for transporting cakes, pies, and tarts.

Finally, you might want to include a recipe or an essential ingredient—such as a bar of bittersweet chocolate or a jar of crystallized ginger—with your gift. Write the recipe on a decorative recipe card or a notecard, or print it out on a sheet of plain or colored paper, roll it up into a scroll, and tie it with a bright ribbon. And enjoy the giving.

1

"thank you" cookies

EVERYBODY LOVES COOKIES, and even people who don't usually bake have been known to make a batch or two. There are lots of easy recipes in this chapter, from Brown Sugar Shortbread (page 42), which takes about five minutes to put together, to Peanut Butter Cookies with Crunch (in several versions; page 26), to slice-and-bake Amazing Toffee Thins (page 30). And there are plenty of cookies that keep and ship well, for those holiday tins or for care packages at any time of the year. In fact, only the two sandwich cookies and the toffee thins are a bit too delicate for long and bumpy journeys.

Tips to Make Your Cookie Baking Even Easier

For best results, use heavy baking sheets—the cookies will bake more evenly, and there is less chance of burning the bottoms (insulated baking sheets seem to give uneven results, so I don't use them). But the recipes give a range for the baking time, so if you are using lightweight pans, just be sure to check on the cookies at the low end of the range. Baking sheets are greased or left ungreased, depending on the recipe. You can use butter (as I do), solid vegetable shortening, or nonstick vegetable spray. Or, if you're a fan of parchment paper (which is now available in most supermarkets), use it to line the baking sheets; it makes cleanup a breeze.

To streamline your production of shaped cookies, such as the Spicy English Gingersnaps (page 32), Peanut Butter Cookies with Crunch (page 26), and Grown-Up Thumbprint Cookies (page 28), portion out the dough for one baking sheet at a time, setting the measured portions on the baking sheet as you go. Then go back and roll each portion into a ball (and finally, depending on the recipe, flatten them or make a "thumbprint" in each one if appropriate). This is much faster than shaping the cookies one at a time—it's always quickest to do one motion (rolling, flattening, etc.) at a time.

Slice-and-bake cookies are especially quick and easy, and in fact the dough for many cookies can be shaped into logs, chilled, and then sliced. I've included a slice-and-bake option only for the Brown Sugar Cut-Out Cookies (page 40), but the dough for almost any drop or rolled cookie, from chocolate chips to sugar cookies, can be shaped this way. In most cases, the baking time will be somewhat less than in the original recipe, since the cookies will be thinner from the start.

Most cookies will keep for at least five days if they are stored in a tin or other tightly sealed container. Key here is to remember to store crisp cookies and soft cookies separately; if you mix them, crisp cookies soon won't be. And just about any plain cookie can be frozen (filled cookies, macaroons, and meringue-type cookies are usually not good candidates) for at least two weeks, convenient when you are doing your holiday baking or making other big batches of cookies. Do be sure to wrap them well so they don't absorb any freezer odors— and label them, so you won't find yourself wondering just what is in all those foil packages (as, I must admit, I sometimes do). For more on storing and wrapping, see pages 17 to 21.

chunky chocolate chip cookies

Makes about 60 cookies

There are times when nothing but a chocolate chip cookie will do. Mine have a lot of chips, and chunks, and/or chopped chocolate—use your favorite combination of mix-ins, for a grand total of up to three cups. Chocolate chip cookie aficionados tend to have strong feelings about texture: For very crisp chocolate chip cookies, bake these for a few minutes longer than indicated; for soft cookies, underbake them slightly.

2¼ cups unbleached all-purpose flour

1 teaspoon baking soda

1 teaspoon salt

½ pound (2 sticks) unsalted butter, at room temperature

¾ cup plus 2 tablespoons granulated sugar

¾ cup plus 2 tablespoons packed dark brown sugar

1½ teaspoons pure vanilla extract

2 large eggs

1 cup semisweet chocolate chips or chunks

¾ to 1 cup milk chocolate chips

*½ to 1 cup mini semisweet chocolate chips or 2 to 4 ounces
    semisweet or bittersweet chocolate, coarsely chopped*

1. Put the racks in the upper and lower thirds of the oven and preheat the oven to 350°F.

2. Whisk together the flour, baking soda, and salt in a medium bowl.

3. In a large bowl, beat the butter and both sugars with an electric mixer on medium speed until light and fluffy, 2 to 3 minutes. Scrape down the sides of the bowl. Beat in the vanilla. Add the eggs one at a time, beating well after each addition. On low speed, beat in the flour mixture in two additions. Using a sturdy wooden spoon, stir in all the chocolate chips.

4. Drop the dough by slightly rounded tablespoonfuls onto ungreased baking sheets, spacing the cookies about 2 inches apart. Bake for 10 to 12 minutes, switching the position of the baking sheets halfway through baking, until the cookies are golden brown around the edges. Let cool on the baking sheets for 1 to 2 minutes, then transfer the cookies to racks to cool completely. *(The cookies can be stored in an airtight container for up to 5 days.)*

peanut butter cookies with crunch

Makes about 60 cookies

For big or little kids—just the thing to send to your homesick college student, or to pack into a school lunch. I'm partial to the bits of peanuts in chunky peanut butter, but creamy is good too. (Use your favorite grocery store peanut butter—"natural" peanut butter doesn't work well for most baking.) If you're a peanut butter cup lover, go straight to the chocolate chip variation.

These are definitely "milk-and-cookie" cookies—or spread your favorite ice cream between the big ones (see the variation) to make "sandwiches." They're fun for kids too: Give them a fork to make the traditional crisscross design on the tops of the cookies.

1½ cups unbleached all-purpose flour

½ teaspoon baking soda

¼ teaspoon salt

8 tablespoons (1 stick) unsalted butter, at room temperature

¾ cup granulated sugar

¼ cup plus 2 tablespoons packed light brown sugar

¾ cup crunchy peanut butter (not "natural style")

1 large egg

1 teaspoon pure vanilla extract

1. Put the racks in the upper and lower thirds of the oven and preheat the oven to 350°F. Grease two large baking sheets.

2. Whisk the flour, baking soda, and salt together in a medium bowl.

3. In a large bowl, beat the butter and both sugars with an electric mixer on medium speed until light and fluffy, 2 to 3 minutes. Scrape down the sides of bowl. Beat in the peanut butter. Beat in the egg, blending well, then beat in the vanilla. On low speed, beat in the flour mixture in two additions.

4. Scoop out a slightly rounded teaspoonful of dough for each cookie, roll the dough into a scant 1-inch ball, and place the balls 2 inches apart on the prepared baking sheets. With the back of a fork, gently press a crisscross pattern into each cookie, flattening it to ¼ inch thick.

5. Bake for 9 to 12 minutes, switching the position of the baking sheets halfway through baking, until the cookies are golden brown on the bottom and barely colored on top. Let cool on the baking sheets for 2 minutes, then transfer the cookies to racks to cool completely. *(The cookies can be stored in an airtight container for up to 5 days.)*

chocolate chip–peanut butter cookies
Stir 1¼ cups mini chocolate chips into the dough. Bake as directed.

jumbo peanut butter cookies
Make the dough as directed, adding chocolate chips as above, if desired. Use a slightly rounded tablespoon of dough for each cookie and flatten each one into a 2¼- to 2½-inch round. Increase the baking time to 10 to 13 minutes. (Makes about 20 cookies)

grown-up thumbprint cookies

Makes about 60 cookies

These thumbprint cookies are filled with an easy, luscious, grown-up chocolate cream.
No Hershey's kisses here! But kids will like them too, of course. You could fill them with the
traditional jelly or jam instead (see the variation)—or make half and half. The rich buttery
cookies are even good plain (flatten the balls of dough slightly with the bottom of a floured
drinking glass and reduce the baking time by a few minutes).

2 cups unbleached all-purpose flour

½ teaspoon baking powder

¼ teaspoon salt

14 tablespoons (1¾ sticks) unsalted
    butter, at room temperature

¾ cup sugar

1 large egg

1¼ teaspoons pure vanilla extract

Chocolate Cream Filling

6 ounces bittersweet or semisweet chocolate,
    finely chopped

¼ cup plus 2 tablespoons heavy cream

1. Put the racks in the upper and lower thirds of the oven and preheat the oven to 350°F.

2. Whisk together the flour, baking powder, and salt in a medium bowl.

3. In a large bowl, beat the butter and sugar with an electric mixer on medium speed until light and fluffy, 2 to 3 minutes. Scrape down the sides of the bowl. Beat in the egg, then beat in the vanilla. On low speed, beat in the flour mixture in two additions.

4. Roll slightly rounded teaspoons of the dough into 1-inch balls and place them 1½ inches apart on ungreased baking sheets. With your thumb, make a deep indentation (almost down to the baking sheet) in the center of each ball.

5. Bake for 10 to 13 minutes, switching the position of the baking sheets halfway through baking, until the cookies are light golden brown. Let cool on the baking sheets for 1 to 2 minutes, then transfer the cookies to wire racks to cool completely. (The cookies can be baked up to 2 days ahead and stored in an airtight container.)

6. FOR THE FILLING: Put the chocolate in a medium bowl. Bring the cream to a boil in a small saucepan. Pour the hot cream over the chocolate and let stand for 30 seconds, then whisk gently until the chocolate is melted and smooth. Let cool, stirring occasionally with a rubber spatula, until the mixture is thickened enough to hold a shape when dropped from a spoon but isn't set, about 45 minutes to 1 hour.

7. Spoon the filling into a small resealable plastic bag, seal the bag, and snip off the tip of one of the bottom corners. (Or, for a more decorative finish, pipe the filling into the cookies using a pastry bag fitted with a medium star tip.) Pipe a dollop of filling into the center of each cookie. Let the cookies stand until the filling has set. (The filled cookies can be stored, layered between sheets of waxed paper, in an airtight container for up to 3 days.)

jam-filled thumbprint cookies

Before baking, fill each cookie with about ¼ teaspoon raspberry or other jam or jelly. The jam will sink a bit as the cookies bake, so if you like, top off the cookies with a little more jam after they've cooled.

 *amazing toffee thins*

Makes 64 cookies

These unusual crisp, buttery cookies don't contain any eggs. They are slice-and-bake, so they are very quick and easy, and the dough is just the thing to keep in the freezer for baking a batch on the spur of the moment. Everyone I know asks for the recipe (here you are, Michelle!).

1¼ cups unbleached all-purpose flour
¼ teaspoon salt
12 tablespoons (1½ sticks) unsalted butter, at room temperature
¾ cup packed dark brown sugar
1½ teaspoons pure vanilla extract

1. Whisk together the flour and salt in a medium bowl.

2. In a large bowl, beat the butter and brown sugar with an electric mixer on medium speed until light and fluffy, 2 to 3 minutes. Scrape down the sides of the bowl. Beat in the vanilla. On low speed, beat in the flour in two additions.

3. Divide the dough in half and put each half on a square of waxed paper. Form each piece into a rough log, wrap loosely in the waxed paper, and refrigerate until firm enough to shape, about 45 minutes.

4. Roll each log of dough under the palms of your hands into an 8-inch-long cylinder (if the dough becomes sticky, refrigerate it briefly), then roll it up tightly in the waxed paper, using the paper to help make a smooth, compact log. Refrigerate until firm, 1½ to 2 hours. *(The dough can be frozen, well wrapped, for up to 1 month. Thaw in the refrigerator before using.)*

5. Put the racks in the upper and lower thirds of the oven and preheat the oven to 350°F.

6. Work with one log of dough at a time, keeping the second one refrigerated. Using a sharp heavy knife, cut the dough into ¼-inch-thick slices and place them about 2 inches apart on ungreased heavy baking sheets (if you don't have heavy baking sheets, reduce the baking time by a minute or two).

7. Bake for 10 to 12 minutes, switching the position of the baking sheets halfway through baking, until the cookies are golden brown around the edges. Let cool on the baking sheets for 3 minutes, then transfer the cookies to racks to cool completely. *(The cookies can be stored in an airtight container for up to 3 days.)*

spicy English gingersnaps

Makes about 96 cookies

Gingersnaps were my father's favorite cookie—perhaps it was his English heritage. While some store-bought gingersnaps aren't bad, these cookies are really, really good. Their secret ingredient is black pepper, though they don't taste at all peppery, just wonderfully spicy. And they are exceptionally easy to make too. A friend who never bakes asked for the recipe as soon as he tasted them and then made them at Christmas. They keep and ship well—slip them into your holiday gift boxes or other care packages, or into the kids' lunch boxes.

These are crisp (that's why they are called snaps); for a slightly chewier cookie, bake them for a minute or so less than indicated.

2 cups unbleached all-purpose flour

2 teaspoons baking soda

2 teaspoons ground ginger

½ teaspoon ground cinnamon

Pinch of ground allspice (optional)

½ teaspoon salt

⅛ teaspoon freshly ground black pepper

12 tablespoons (1½ sticks) unsalted butter, at room temperature

½ cup granulated sugar, plus about 1 cup for rolling

½ cup packed light brown sugar

1 large egg

¼ cup dark molasses

1. Whisk together the flour, baking soda, ginger, cinnamon, allspice, if using, salt, and pepper in a medium bowl.

2. In a large bowl, beat the butter and both sugars with an electric mixer on medium speed until light and fluffy, 2 to 3 minutes. Scrape down the sides of the bowl. Beat in the egg, blending well, then beat in the molasses. On low speed, beat in the flour mixture in two additions. Cover and refrigerate until the dough is firm enough to shape, about 2 hours. *(The dough can be refrigerated for up to 1 day; it can also be frozen, well wrapped, for up to 2 weeks. Thaw in the refrigerator before using.)*

3. Put the racks in the upper and lower thirds of the oven and preheat the oven to 350°F. Grease two heavy baking sheets (if you don't have heavy baking sheets, reduce the baking time by a minute or two).

4. Put the sugar for rolling in a small shallow bowl. Using about 1 level teaspoon of dough per cookie, roll the dough into scant 1-inch balls, then roll the balls in the sugar, coating well, and place 2 inches apart on the prepared baking sheets.

5. Bake for 9 to 11 minutes, switching the position of the baking sheets halfway through baking, until the cookies are flat and crinkled and the edges are very slightly browned. Let cool on the baking sheets for 1 to 2 minutes, then transfer the cookies to racks to cool completely. *(The cookies can be stored in an airtight container for up to 5 days.)*

melt-in-your-mouth coconut macaroons

Makes about 60 cookies

These sweet, chewy macaroons are pure bliss for the coconut lover. Add chopped chocolate or chips (see the variation) and you've got a cookie version of a Mounds bar. (If your ideal macaroon is almond-flavored, add ½ teaspoon pure almond extract and reduce the vanilla to 1 teaspoon.)

3 large egg whites, at room temperature
Pinch of salt
1 cup sugar
1½ teaspoons pure vanilla extract
One 7-ounce package (2¾ cups) sweetened shredded coconut

1. Put the racks in the upper and lower thirds of the oven and preheat the oven to 325°F. Line two to four heavy baking sheets with aluminum foil.

2. In a large bowl, beat the egg whites with an electric mixer on medium speed until foamy. Beat in the salt. Increase the speed to medium high and beat until the whites start to hold soft peaks. Gradually add the sugar, about 1 tablespoon at a time, and continue to beat until the whites hold firm, glossy peaks. Using a large rubber spatula, fold in the vanilla, then fold in the coconut, breaking up any large clumps of coconut as you add it to the bowl.

3. Drop the batter by heaping teaspoonfuls onto the prepared baking sheets, spacing the cookies about 1½ inches apart. Bake for 15 to 17 minutes, switching the position of the baking sheets halfway through baking, until the macaroons are lightly golden and feel just set when touched. Transfer the baking sheets to wire racks and let the cookies cool completely. (If you have only two baking sheets, let the cookies cool for 2 to 3 minutes on the sheets, then transfer them, on the foil, to racks to cool while you bake the remaining cookies; be sure to let the baking sheets cool completely between batches.)

4. Carefully peel the cooled cookies off the foil. *(The cookies can be stored in an airtight container for up to 5 days.)*

 ## chocolate chip coconut macaroons

After folding in the coconut, fold in 5 ounces bittersweet or semisweet chocolate, coarsely chopped, or a scant 1 cup mini chocolate chips. If you are using chopped chocolate, be sure to add any "crumbs" from chopping the chocolate as well; they will give the macaroons an attractive, lightly speckled appearance.

chocolate espresso sandwich cookies

Makes about 30 sandwich cookies

These sophisticated sandwich cookies are filled with an espresso-flavored chocolate cream. Because there's instant espresso coffee powder (it's available in most supermarkets) in the dough too, the unfilled cookies are quite nice on their own (but reduce the amount of espresso powder to 1½ teaspoons—without the chocolate filling to balance it, the coffee flavor seems stronger). Either way, these are an unusual treat.

1 cup unbleached all-purpose flour
¼ cup unsweetened cocoa powder (not Dutch-processed; see page 12)
½ teaspoon baking soda
⅛ teaspoon salt
1¾ teaspoons instant espresso coffee powder (such as Medaglia d'Oro)
1½ teaspoons pure vanilla extract
8 tablespoons (1 stick) unsalted butter, at room temperature
½ cup granulated sugar
½ cup packed light brown sugar
1 large egg

Chocolate Espresso Cream Filling

5 ounces bittersweet or semisweet chocolate, coarsely chopped
¼ cup plus 1 tablespoon heavy cream
½ teaspoon instant espresso coffee powder

1. Put the racks in the upper and lower thirds of the oven and preheat the oven to 350°F. Lightly grease two baking sheets.

2. Whisk together the flour, cocoa powder, baking soda, and salt in a medium bowl. Combine the espresso powder and vanilla in a small cup and stir until the espresso powder is completely dissolved.

3. In a large bowl, beat the butter and both sugars with an electric mixer on medium speed until light and creamy, 2 to 3 minutes. Scrape down the sides of the bowl. Beat in the egg, blending well. Beat in the espresso mixture. On low speed, beat in the flour mixture in three additions.

4. Drop the dough by slightly rounded teaspoonfuls onto the prepared baking sheets, spacing the cookies about 1½ inches apart. Bake for 9 to 11 minutes, switching the position of the baking sheets halfway through baking, until the edges of the cookies are lightly browned but the centers are still slightly soft. (For crisper cookies, bake for about 2 minutes longer.) Let cool on the baking sheets for 1 to 2 minutes, then transfer the cookies to wire racks to cool completely. *(The cookies can be stored in an airtight container for up to 3 days.)*

5. **FOR THE FILLING:** Put the chocolate in a food processor and process until finely chopped. Combine the cream and espresso powder in a small saucepan and bring to a boil, stirring to dissolve the espresso powder. With the machine running, add the cream to the processor and process just until the chocolate is completely melted, stopping once or twice to scrape down the sides of the bowl. Transfer the filling to another bowl and let stand at room temperature, stirring occasionally with a rubber spatula, until cooled and thickened to a spreadable consistency, about 30 minutes.

6. To assemble the cookies, turn half the cookies upside down and spread a slightly rounded teaspoonful of filling on the bottom of each one, leaving about a ¼-inch border all around. Top with the remaining cookies, right side up, and gently press them together. Let stand for about 30 minutes to set the filling. *(The cookies can be stored in an airtight container for up to 1 day.)*

raspberry linzer hearts

Makes about 34 sandwich cookies

For Valentine's Day, of course, or anytime. These cookies are sandwiched with raspberry preserves and have a delicate, almost crumbly texture. They are traditionally filled with raspberry preserves with seeds, but seedless preserves are excellent too. And although the recipe calls for a heart-shaped cutter, you can always make the cookies round instead (see Note).

1 cup unblanched whole almonds
2¼ cups unbleached all-purpose flour
¾ teaspoon ground cinnamon
⅛ teaspoon ground cloves
¼ teaspoon salt
½ pound (2 sticks) unsalted butter, at room temperature
¾ cup confectioners' sugar, plus extra for dusting
2 large egg yolks
1 teaspoon grated lemon zest
About ¾ cup raspberry preserves

1. Combine the almonds and ½ cup of the flour in a food processor and process until the almonds are finely ground (be sure to grind the nuts very fine or the cookies may be too crumbly). Add the remaining 1¾ cups flour, the cinnamon, cloves, and salt and process until thoroughly mixed.

2. In a large bowl (use a stand mixer if you have one), beat the butter and confectioners' sugar with an electric mixer on medium speed until light and fluffy, 2 to 3 minutes. Scrape down the sides of the bowl. Add the egg yolks one at a time, beating well after each addition. Beat in the lemon zest. On low speed, beat in the flour mixture in three additions.

3. Divide the dough into quarters, shape each quarter into a disk, and wrap individually in plastic wrap. Refrigerate for 1 to 2 hours, or until firm enough to roll. *(The dough can be refrigerated for up to 1 day.)*

4. Put the racks in the upper and lower thirds of the oven and preheat the oven to 350°F.

5. On a well-floured surface, using a floured rolling pin, roll out one piece of dough approximately 1/8 inch thick. Cut out cookies with a 2½-inch heart-shaped cutter and, using a metal spatula, transfer the cookies, as you cut them, to an ungreased baking sheet, spacing them about 1 inch apart. Set the baking sheet aside for the moment; wrap the dough scraps in plastic and refrigerate. Roll out a second piece of dough, cut out more cookies, and transfer to another ungreased baking sheet. Using a 3/4- to 1-inch heart-shaped cutter, cut out the centers of the cookies on the second baking sheet. If desired, transfer a few of the cut-out heart centers to the baking sheet with the uncut cookies; add the (remaining) centers to the other dough scraps.

6. Bake the cookies for 9 to 12 minutes, switching the position of the baking sheets halfway through baking, until the edges are just starting to brown. The cut-out cookies will take slightly less time to bake than the whole cookies. Let cool on the baking sheets for about 1 minute, then transfer the cookies to wire racks to cool completely. Repeat with the remaining dough, then reroll the scraps once to make more cookies, keeping in mind that you want to make an equal number of whole and cut-out cookies.

7. **TO ASSEMBLE THE COOKIES:** If the preserves are cold, stir them in a small cup until smooth. Spread 1 scant teaspoon preserves evenly over the top of each whole cookie. Generously dust the cut-out cookies with confectioners' sugar and place them on top of the raspberry-covered cookies. *(The cookies can be stored between layers of waxed paper in an airtight container for up to 5 days.)* If you baked them, the small heart cookies can be enjoyed as a cook's treat or used as a garnish on a plate of the linzer cookies.

NOTE: For round cookies, use a 2-inch round cutter, preferably a scalloped one, to cut out the cookies and a 3/4-inch plain round cutter (use the wide end of a pastry tip if you don't have a tiny round cutter) to cut out the centers. (Makes about 40 cookies)

brown sugar cut-out cookies

Makes about fifty 3-inch-long cookies

These playful cookies are perfect for your gift tins at holiday time, though I make them, in one version or another, all year round. Use traditional cutters—stars, snowmen, reindeer, etc.—or whatever strikes your fancy. I've even made cats and dogs for my friends at my vet's office.

If you want to hang the cookies on the Christmas tree, before baking, make a ¼-inch hole in the top of each one with a skewer or straw, then use narrow red ribbon to hang them. If you like, decorate the cookies with the easy confectioners' sugar icing (recipe follows), but they're very good plain. And if you're too busy to make cut-out cookies, the dough can be shaped into slice-and-bake logs (see the variation).

2 cups unbleached all-purpose flour
1 teaspoon baking powder
¼ teaspoon salt
12 tablespoons (1½ sticks) unsalted butter,
    at room temperature
1 cup packed dark brown sugar
1 large egg
1 teaspoon pure vanilla extract

1. Whisk together the flour, baking powder, and salt in a medium bowl.

2. In a large bowl, beat the butter and brown sugar with an electric mixer on medium speed until light and fluffy, 2 to 3 minutes. Scrape down the sides of the bowl. Beat in the egg, then beat in the vanilla. On low speed, beat in the flour mixture in two additions. Divide the dough into quarters, shape each piece into a disk, and wrap individually in plastic wrap. Refrigerate for 2 hours, or until firm enough to roll. (*The dough can be refrigerated for up to 1 day; it can also be frozen, well wrapped, for up to 1 month. Thaw in the refrigerator before using.*)

3. Put the racks in the upper and lower thirds of the oven and preheat the oven to 350°F.

4. On a lightly floured surface, roll out the dough one piece at a time to a scant ¼ inch thick. Cut out cookies with cookie cutters and place them 1½ inches apart on ungreased baking sheets. Gather the scraps together and reroll once to make more cookies.

5. Bake for 8 to 10 minutes, switching the position of the baking sheets halfway through baking, until the edges of the cookies are very lightly browned. Let cool on the baking sheets for about 1 minute, then transfer the cookies to wire racks to cool completely. (*The cookies can be stored in an airtight container for up to 5 days.*)

 ## slice-and-bake brown sugar cookies

Divide the dough in half and shape each half into an 8-inch-long log (if the dough is very soft, refrigerate it briefly before shaping). Wrap in plastic wrap and freeze until firm, at least 1 hour (the dough can be frozen, well wrapped, for up to 2 weeks). Using a sharp knife, cut the logs into scant ¼-inch-thick slices and arrange them 1½ inches apart on ungreased baking sheets. Bake as directed. (Makes about 80 cookies)

Confectioners' Sugar Icing

Put 1 cup confectioners' sugar in a small bowl and stir in just enough water to make a smooth icing. If desired, divide the icing between two (or more) small bowls and tint it with different food colors. (Makes about ½ cup)

To decorate the cookies with the icing, transfer the icing to a small resealable plastic bag, cut off the tip of one bottom corner of the bag, and pipe designs onto the cookies. Or, instead of piping the icing, make a double batch of icing, tint it various colors, and spread it on the cookies. Let the icing set before storing the cookies, layering them between sheets of waxed paper.

brown sugar shortbread

Makes 36 cookies

These couldn't be quicker or easier. No need to chill the dough or roll it out, you just mix it, pat it into the pan, and bake. And the cookies are incredibly delicious (these are the Cat Doctor's very favorite cookie, and he's a shortbread connoisseur). They have a slight caramel undertone from the brown sugar and a delightfully crumbly texture; when someone who tasted them wondered how I could make butter have the texture of a cookie, I took it as a compliment. If you've never made cookies before, start with these.

½ pound (2 sticks) unsalted butter,
    at room temperature
⅓ cup granulated sugar
⅓ cup packed brown sugar
1 teaspoon pure vanilla extract
⅛ teaspoon salt
2 cups unbleached all-purpose flour

1. Put a rack in the middle of the oven and preheat the oven to 325°F.

2. In a large bowl, beat the butter and both sugars with an electric mixer on medium speed just until thoroughly blended, about 1 minute. Scrape down the sides of the bowl. Beat in the vanilla, then beat in the salt. On low speed, add the flour in two additions, beating just until incorporated.

3. Turn the dough out into an ungreased 9-by-13-inch baking pan and, with your fingertips and/or a sturdy rubber spatula, gently press it evenly over the bottom of the pan. Bake for 50 to 55 minutes, or until the shortbread is golden brown (the edges will be slightly darker); do not underbake. Let cool in the pan on a wire rack for 5 to 10 minutes.

4. With a sharp heavy knife, cut the shortbread, still in the pan, into 36 rectangles. Let cool completely before removing the shortbread from the pan. *(The shortbread can be stored in an airtight container for up to 5 days.)*

ginger-ginger petticoat tails

Makes 32 cookies

These shortbread triangles ("petticoat tails" is their traditional Scottish name) are studded with sweet-spicy bits of candied ginger. Buy the crystallized ginger sold in bulk at specialty markets—it's both better and much less expensive than what you'll find in jars at the supermarket.

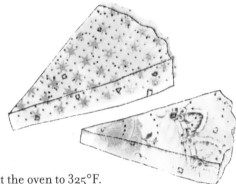

2 cups unbleached all-purpose flour

¼ teaspoon salt

¼ teaspoon ground ginger

½ pound (2 sticks) unsalted butter,
  at room temperature

⅔ cup sugar

½ cup finely minced crystallized ginger

1. Put a rack in the middle of the oven and preheat the oven to 325°F.

2. Whisk together the flour, salt, and ground ginger in a medium bowl.

3. In a large bowl, beat the butter and sugar with an electric mixer on medium speed just until thoroughly blended, about 1 minute. Scrape down the sides of the bowl. Beat in the crystallized ginger. On low speed, add the flour mixture in two additions, beating just until incorporated.

4. Divide the dough in half. With your fingertips and/or a sturdy rubber spatula, press each half evenly into the bottom of an ungreased 9-inch round cake pan. With a fork, make a decorative border all around the edge of each round of dough.

5. Bake for 45 to 50 minutes, until the shortbread is golden brown (the edges will be slightly darker); do not underbake. Let cool in the pans on a wire rack for 5 to 10 minutes.

6. With a sharp heavy knife, cut each round of shortbread, still in the pans, into 16 wedges. Let cool completely before removing the wedges from the pans. *(The shortbread can be stored in an airtight container for up to 5 days.)*

sweet baby lemon scones

Makes about 26 scones

These diminutive scones aren't really cookies, of course, but they are a lovely treat at breakfast, or anytime. Although they are tempting warm from the oven, they are even better if they're allowed to mellow overnight—give a batch to a friend in need of a relaxing breakfast in bed. The dried cherry or blueberry version (see the variation) is a riff on old-fashioned currant tea scones. Or, if you omit the lemon zest in the basic recipe, you will have classic cream scones. These are so buttery, however, that there's no need for the clotted cream traditionally served alongside.

2 cups unbleached all-purpose flour

1/3 cup sugar

1 tablespoon baking powder

1/2 teaspoon salt

1 tablespoon grated lemon zest

8 tablespoons (1 stick) unsalted
butter, cut into 1/4-inch cubes
and chilled

3/4 cup heavy cream, plus
1 to 2 tablespoons for brushing

1. Put the racks in the upper and lower thirds of the oven and preheat the oven to 425°F. Grease two baking sheets.

2. Whisk together the flour, sugar, baking powder, and salt in a large bowl. Whisk in the lemon zest. Using a pastry blender, two knives, or your fingertips, cut in the butter until it is in pieces no larger than tiny peas. Using a fork, stir in the cream just until a shaggy dough forms.

3. Turn the dough out onto a lightly floured surface and knead briefly, just until it comes together; do not overwork. Pat the dough into a $^3/_4$-inch-thick disk. With a $1^1/_2$-inch round biscuit cutter, cut out as many rounds as possible from the dough and place them $1^1/_2$ inches apart on the prepared baking sheets. Gather the scraps of dough and knead together gently, then pat out and cut out more scones. Lightly brush the tops of the scones with cream.

4. Bake for 12 to 14 minutes, switching the position of the baking sheets halfway through baking, until the scones are risen and golden brown. Transfer to wire racks to cool slightly and serve warm, or let cool to room temperature. (*The scones can be stored in an airtight container for up to 1 day. If you like, reheat them, loosely wrapped in foil, in a 350°F oven for about 10 minutes.*)

 ## *baby scones with dried cherries or blueberries*

Omit the lemon zest. Add $^1/_2$ cup dried cherries or blueberries, coarsely chopped, to the dough when you knead it. Proceed as directed.

2

brownies and bars for your favorite people

BROWNIES AND BARS can be among the easiest cookies to make: Just spread the batter in the pan and bake, and you've made a lot of cookies all at once. Both the Very Special Fudgy Brownies (page 48) and the Refined Chocolate Coconut Bars (page 52) fit into the quick-and-easy category. And bars like brownies are definitely comfort food, treats that you've enjoyed since childhood. But when you dress them up with various toppings or fillings, they become an elegant indulgence (the brownies can be made sophisticated simply by cutting them into diminutive sweet bites). Even so, they are usually still quick and easy to make and rarely require much more in the way of equipment than a baking pan, a bowl or two, and a hand mixer.

All of these brownies and bars travel well. For easy transport, you can leave them in the pan after you've cut them: Just cover the pan tightly with foil. Or layer them in a tin, between sheets of waxed paper if they are topped or filled, or wrap them in plastic wrap and foil, either individually or in stacks. (Maida Heatter, "the Cookie Queen," always carries a few brownies in her purse, ready to give to friends or other "important people.") And all of these brownies and bars can be frozen, well wrapped, for up to two weeks.

very special fudgy brownies

Makes 48 brownies

After good friends surprised me with a three-pound slab of Scharffen Berger special "70% cacao bittersweet chocolate," I had what I needed to create what have become my all-time favorite fudgy brownies. I now make them almost weekly to give to someone for one reason or another (for me, chocolate is both a celebration and a solace). And the recipe makes a lot, so I get to freeze a few for myself from each batch. The chocolate shards, chunks, or chips—use your favorite—provide unexpected bursts of deep chocolate flavor. While the chocolate melts as the brownies bake, it doesn't dissolve into the batter, and if the brownies are not chilled (other than briefly, for easier cutting), the chocolate stays soft, almost gooey, if you use chopped chocolate bars. For a different texture, though, you can chill the brownies thoroughly, and the chunks will be firm and . . . chunky.

For a less intense version, omit the chopped chocolate or chips. These plain brownies are also very good cold. For more demure servings, cut these into one-inch squares (you'll have ninety-six little brownie bites).

> $\frac{1}{2}$ pound (2 sticks) unsalted butter, cut into chunks
>
> 6 ounces high-quality unsweetened chocolate (see page 12), coarsely chopped
>
> 2 ounces bittersweet chocolate, coarsely chopped
>
> 4 large eggs
>
> $1\frac{3}{4}$ cups granulated sugar
>
> $\frac{1}{2}$ cup packed light brown sugar
>
> $\frac{1}{4}$ teaspoon salt
>
> $1\frac{1}{2}$ teaspoons pure vanilla extract
>
> 1 cup unbleached all-purpose flour
>
> 7 ounces bittersweet or semisweet chocolate, coarsely chopped or
> cut into shards (see page 13), or $1\frac{1}{2}$ cups semisweet chocolate chunks
> or large semisweet chocolate chips

1. Put a rack in the middle of the oven and preheat the oven to 350°F. Line a 9-by-13-inch baking pan with foil, leaving an overhang on the narrow ends.

2. Combine the butter, unsweetened chocolate, and 2 ounces bittersweet chocolate in a medium heavy saucepan and melt over low heat, stirring frequently until smooth. Remove from the heat.

3. In a large bowl, beat the eggs and both sugars with an electric mixer on low speed just until smooth. Beat in the salt. Beat in the melted chocolate mixture, then beat in the vanilla. Scrape down the sides of the bowl. Beat in the flour in two additions (the batter will be thick). Stir in the 7 ounces chocolate.

4. Scrape the batter into the prepared pan and smooth the top. Bake for 23 to 25 minutes, or until the top is set but still soft and the edges are puffed and just beginning to pull away from the sides of the pan. A toothpick inserted in the center will come out still gooey (be brave!—underbaking the brownies is one of the secrets to their fudgy texture). Transfer the pan to a wire rack to cool completely.

5. For the neatest cuts, refrigerate the pan for about 20 minutes before cutting the brownies. Using the foil, lift the brownie slab out of the pan. Carefully peel off the foil and put the brownie on a large cutting board. With a large sharp knife, cut the brownie into 48 squares. *(The brownies can be stored in an airtight container at room temperature for up to 3 days; they can also be frozen, well wrapped, for up to 2 weeks.)*

caramel-topped turtle brownies

Makes 36 brownies

Topped with a layer of creamy caramel and pecans and then drizzled with chocolate, these brownies are cousins of the candies known as turtles. Hershey's caramels really make the creamiest topping, but the brownies are still delicious if you must substitute cellophane-wrapped square caramels (you'll need fewer of them, about thirty-six). My mother makes these whenever she's asked to bring dessert.

> 12 tablespoons (1½ sticks) unsalted butter
>
> 3 ounces high-quality unsweetened chocolate (see page 12), coarsely chopped
>
> 3 large eggs
>
> 1 cup granulated sugar
>
> ½ cup packed light brown sugar
>
> ¼ teaspoon salt
>
> 1½ teaspoons pure vanilla extract
>
> ½ cup plus 2 tablespoons unbleached all-purpose flour

Caramel Topping

45 Hershey's caramels (about 10 ounces)

½ cup heavy cream

Generous 2 cups (about 8½ ounces) pecan halves

Drizzle

2 ounces semisweet chocolate, coarsely chopped

3 tablespoons heavy cream

1. Put a rack in the middle of the oven and preheat the oven to 350°F. Grease a 9-by-13-inch baking pan.

2. Combine the butter and chocolate in a medium heavy saucepan and melt over low heat, stirring frequently until smooth. Remove from the heat.

3. In a large bowl, beat the eggs and both sugars with an electric mixer on low speed just until smooth. Beat in the salt. Beat in the melted chocolate mixture, then beat in the vanilla. Scrape down the sides of the bowl. On low speed, beat in the flour in two additions.

4. Scrape the batter into the prepared pan and smooth the top. Bake for 20 to 22 minutes, until just firm to the touch. Transfer the pan to a wire rack.

5. MEANWHILE, FOR THE TOPPING: Melt the caramels with the cream in a large heavy saucepan over low heat, stirring frequently, until smooth. Add the pecans and stir until well coated.

6. Scrape the topping onto the hot brownie layer, gently spreading it evenly. Let cool on the rack, then refrigerate the brownie for 1 hour, or until the topping is chilled and set.

7. FOR THE DRIZZLE: Combine the chocolate and cream in a small heavy saucepan and heat over low heat, stirring frequently, until melted and smooth. Using a fork, drizzle or spatter the chocolate over the bars in a zigzag pattern. Refrigerate for 30 minutes, or until the chocolate is set.

8. Using a sharp heavy knife, cut the brownie, in the pan, into 36 bars. Serve chilled or at room temperature. *(The bars can be refrigerated, tightly covered, for up to 5 days; they can also be frozen, well wrapped, for up to 2 weeks.)*

 *refined chocolate coconut bars*

Makes 48 bars

An upscale version of those chewy, sweet coconut bars from childhood, known as magic cookie bars or hello Dollys, among other names. Here, chopped high-quality bittersweet or semisweet chocolate (see page 12) stands in for the chocolate chips (I skipped the butterscotch bits), and crushed shortbread cookies replace the graham cracker crumbs (Lorna Doones are fine, but you could also splurge on the imported Scottish cookies). Use any good chocolate, but it's easiest to cut 3½-ounce bars into shards. I admit that I did leave the canned sweetened condensed milk— the recipe just wouldn't be the same without it. (When my friend Catherine serves these at one of her soigné dessert parties, they always disappear first.)

10 tablespoons (1¼ sticks) unsalted butter

1²⁄₃ cups shortbread cookie crumbs

1¾ cups sweetened flaked coconut

1 cup pecans, coarsely chopped (optional)

7 ounces bittersweet or semisweet chocolate, cut into ¾-by-¼-inch shards
   (see page 13) or coarsely chopped

One 14-ounce can sweetened condensed milk

1. Put a rack in the middle of the oven and preheat the oven to 350°F.

2. Melt the butter in a small saucepan. Pour the butter into a 9-by-13-inch baking pan, tilting the pan so the butter covers the entire bottom. Sprinkle the cookie crumbs evenly over the bottom of the pan. Sprinkle ½ cup of the coconut over the crumbs, then scatter the nuts, if using, over the coconut. Scatter the chocolate over the top, then sprinkle the remaining coconut over the chocolate. Drizzle the condensed milk evenly over the top.

3. Bake for 20 to 25 minutes, until the coconut is golden brown in spots and the condensed milk is bubbling (the bars will firm up as they cool). Transfer the pan to a wire rack to cool completely.

4. To make cutting easier, refrigerate the pan briefly. Using a large sharp knife, cut the bar, in the pan, into 48 squares. Serve at room temperature or chilled. *(The bars can be stored in an airtight container at room temperature for up to 3 days or refrigerated for up to 5 days; they can also be frozen, well wrapped, for up to 2 weeks.)*

lemon coconut bars

Makes 24 bars

Coconut is a great addition to traditional lemon bars: Its sweetness sets off the citrus tang, and the chewy coconut contrasts nicely with the smooth lemon topping.

Shortbread Crust	**Lemon Coconut Filling**
$\frac{1}{2}$ pound (2 sticks) unsalted butter, at room temperature	4 large eggs
$\frac{1}{2}$ cup confectioners' sugar	$1\frac{1}{4}$ cups granulated sugar
1 tablespoon grated lemon zest	$\frac{1}{4}$ cup unbleached all-purpose flour
Scant $\frac{1}{4}$ teaspoon salt	$\frac{1}{2}$ teaspoon baking powder
2 cups unbleached all-purpose flour	1 tablespoon grated lemon zest
	$\frac{1}{4}$ cup plus 2 tablespoons fresh lemon juice
	One 7-ounce package ($2\frac{3}{4}$ cups) sweetened shredded coconut

1. Put a rack in the middle of the oven and preheat the oven to 350°F. Line a 9-by-13-inch baking pan with aluminum foil, allowing the foil to extend over the narrow ends of the pan. Grease just the sides of the foil.

2. **FOR THE CRUST:** In a large bowl, beat the butter and confectioners' sugar with an electric mixer on medium speed until thoroughly blended. Beat in the lemon zest, then beat in the salt. On low speed, beat in the flour in two additions. Press the crust mixture evenly over the bottom of the prepared pan. Bake for 15 to 18 minutes, until the crust is golden around the edges.

3. **WHILE THE CRUST BAKES, MAKE THE TOPPING:** In a large bowl, beat the eggs with the mixer on low speed until foamy. Beat in the sugar. Beat in the flour and baking powder, then beat in the lemon zest and juice. Stir in the coconut, breaking up any clumps with your fingers.

4. Scrape the topping onto the hot prebaked crust, spreading the coconut evenly. Bake for 25 to 28 minutes, until the topping is lightly colored and the edges are golden brown. Transfer the pan to a wire rack to cool completely.

5. For easier cutting, refrigerate just until chilled. Invert the bar onto a baking sheet and peel off the foil. Invert again onto a cutting board and, using a sharp knife, cut into 24 squares. *(The bars can be stored in an airtight container at room temperature for up to 1 day or refrigerated for up to 2 days; they can also be frozen, well wrapped, for up to 2 weeks.)*

ganache-filled brown sugar bars

Makes 48 bars

Ganache is the somewhat ungainly French word for the delicious—and very versatile—mixture of chocolate and cream that, depending on the proportion of chocolate to cream, can be used as a filling, frosting, or glaze, as well as for making truffles. (You'll come across different versions of ganache in other desserts in this book, including the Grown-Up Thumbprint Cookies, page 28, and the Whipped Chocolate Tart, page 89.) These bars are perfectly portable because their "frosting" is inside, not on top (for ganache-topped bars, see the variation).

Who knew that little boys love ganache? My friend Ellen's sons, Sam and Peter, have requested these instead of cake for their birthdays ever since they were small. (Big boys like them too; these are the Cat Doctor's all-time favorite.)

1¾ cups unbleached all-purpose flour

¼ teaspoon salt

½ pound (2 sticks) unsalted butter,
    at room temperature

1¾ cups packed dark brown sugar

2 large eggs

1½ teaspoons pure vanilla extract

Chocolate Ganache

8 ounces bittersweet or semisweet
    chocolate, coarsely chopped

½ cup heavy cream

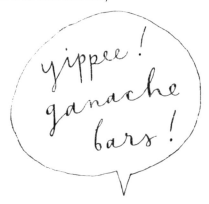

1. Put a rack in the middle of the oven and preheat the oven to 350°F. Line a 10-by-15-inch baking pan with aluminum foil, letting the foil extend about 1 inch over the narrow ends of the pan.

2. Whisk together the flour and salt in a medium bowl.

3. In a large bowl, beat the butter and brown sugar with an electric mixer on medium speed until light and fluffy, 2 to 3 minutes. Scrape down the sides of the bowl. Add the eggs one at a time, beating well after each addition. Beat in the vanilla. On low speed, beat in the flour mixture in two additions (the batter will be stiff).

4. Spoon large dollops of the batter into the prepared pan, then use a long metal spatula to spread the batter evenly. Bake for 18 to 20 minutes, or until a toothpick inserted in the center comes out clean but not dry; do not overbake. Transfer the pan to a rack to cool completely.

5. **MEANWHILE, FOR THE GANACHE:** Put the chocolate in a food processor and process until finely chopped. Bring the cream to a boil in a medium saucepan. With the machine running, add the cream to the processor and process just until the chocolate is completely melted, stopping once or twice to scrape down the sides of the bowl. Scrape the ganache into a medium bowl and let stand, stirring occasionally with a rubber spatula, until cooled and thickened to a spreadable consistency, 45 minutes to 1 hour.

6. Cover the pan with a large wire rack (or a baking sheet) and invert the brown sugar layer onto the rack. Peel off the foil and invert the layer onto a large cutting board. Using a long serrated knife, cut the layer crosswise in half. Using a long metal spatula, spread the ganache evenly over one half of the layer, leaving a ⅛-inch border all around. Carefully set the other half on top, aligning the cut edges. Cover loosely with foil or plastic wrap and refrigerate until the ganache is set, at least 2 hours.

7. Using a long serrated knife, trim the uncut edges of the layers. Cut the layers lengthwise into 6 strips, then cut each strip into 8 bars. Serve chilled or at room temperature. (*The bars can be refrigerated in an airtight container for up to 3 days; they can also be frozen, well wrapped, for up to 2 weeks.*)

inside-out brown sugar bars

Make a double recipe of ganache, using 1 pound bittersweet or semisweet chocolate and 1 cup heavy cream. (This will take a bit longer to set to spreadable consistency.) Trim the edges of the brown sugar layer, but do not cut it in half. Spread the ganache evenly over the top of the layer and refrigerate until set, at least 2 hours. Cut it crosswise in half, then cut each half lengthwise into 4 or 6 strips, and cut each strip into 6 or 8 rectangles. (Makes 48 large or 96 smaller bars)

easy raspberry linzer squares

Makes 20 to 25 bars

These are made with a rich, buttery almond dough and filled with high-quality preserves or jam. Raspberry preserves (not seedless) are traditional, but you could use other berry preserves or even apricot, which is a nice match with the almonds. The lattice topping is classic, but there's no need to weave the strips of dough together—just arrange them in a crisscross pattern.

1 cup whole unblanched almonds
1 cup granulated sugar
1½ cups unbleached all-purpose flour
1 teaspoon baking powder
¼ teaspoon salt
½ teaspoon ground cinnamon
Pinch of ground cloves

14 tablespoons (1¾ sticks) unsalted butter,
* at room temperature*
1 large egg
¾ teaspoon pure vanilla extract
1 teaspoon grated lemon zest
½ cup raspberry preserves or jam
Confectioners' sugar for dusting

1. Put a rack in the middle of the oven and preheat the oven to 350°F.

2. Combine the almonds and 2 tablespoons of the granulated sugar in a food processor and pulse for about 30 seconds, or until the almonds are finely ground; do not process to a paste. Add the flour, baking powder, salt, cinnamon, and cloves and process for about 10 seconds, until thoroughly mixed.

3. In a large bowl, beat the butter and the remaining ¾ cup plus 2 tablespoons sugar with an electric mixer on medium speed until light and fluffy, 2 to 3 minutes. Scrape down the sides of the bowl. Beat in the egg, blending well. Beat in the vanilla and lemon zest. On low speed, beat in the flour mixture in two additions (the dough will be stiff).

4. Measure out 1 cup of the dough for the topping, put it on a sheet of waxed paper, and pat it out into a 6-inch square. Cover the square with a second sheet of waxed paper, place it on a small baking sheet, and put it in the freezer to firm up.

5. Pat the remaining dough evenly over the bottom of an ungreased 8-inch square baking pan. Stir the preserves to loosen them slightly, then spoon them over the dough and spread them evenly to the edges with a rubber spatula. Set aside.

6. When the chilled dough is firm to the touch, roll it out, still between the sheets of waxed paper, to an 8- to 8½-inch square. Peel off the top sheet of paper, then replace it (this will make removing the cut strips of dough from the paper easier), flip the square of dough over, and peel off the top sheet of paper. With a sharp knife, trim the edges of the square to even them and cut the dough into 12 strips.

7. Arrange 6 strips of dough over the preserves, spacing them evenly (if any of the strips tear, just patch them with your fingertips; if the dough becomes too soft to work with, return it briefly to the freezer). Arrange the remaining strips across the first ones, spacing them evenly.

8. Bake for 35 to 38 minutes, or until the dough is deep golden brown. Transfer the pan to a rack to cool completely.

9. Sift confectioners' sugar over the top of the linzer bars. Using a sharp knife, cut the square, in the pan, into 20 to 25 bars. (*The bars can be stored in an airtight container for up to 3 days; they can also be frozen, well wrapped, for up to 2 weeks.*)

3

I baked you a cake

MAKING A CAKE from scratch is almost as easy as using a mix—really!—and the results are so much better (after all, you still have to butter and flour the pans, the only part I find tedious, when using a mix). There are just a few simple tips to keep in mind for perfect results.

Measuring flour accurately is always important in baking, but especially so here. Some books instruct you to spoon the flour into the measuring cup before leveling off the top, but that doesn't match the reality of how most people bake, so I used the "dip-and-scoop" method for all of these recipes: First, stir the flour in the container to aerate it, then scoop up a heaping measuring-cup full and level the top with the back of a knife. It is important not to pack the flour into the cup as you scoop—and don't tap the cup on the counter to level the top, which would also pack the flour down. If you use too much flour, your cake may be dry or dense.

The butter must be at room temperature, which means soft to the touch but not so soft that your finger mashes the butter when you touch it (in this case, softer is not better— if the butter is too warm, the cake may taste greasy). When I'm in a hurry, I cut the butter into thin slices and scatter them over the bottom of the mixing bowl so they will warm up quickly. Don't use the microwave, because you are likely to end up melting at least a bit of it.

For most cake recipes, the butter and sugar are "creamed together," that is, beaten until light and fluffy, or creamy. This step is essential for both the texture and structure of the cake, so it's important not to skimp on the beating time, two to three minutes in most cases. Scrape down the sides of the bowl once or twice with a rubber spatula so all the ingredients are thoroughly blended. Then add the eggs one at a time, mixing well and scraping down the sides of the bowl again if necessary. Finally, add the flour and liquid and other remaining ingredients, beating just until thoroughly mixed.

Some of these recipes specify cooling the cake layers upside down. If the center has risen much more than the edge, cooling the layer upside down will yield a more level layer. But how the layers are cooled depends on the recipe—for some cakes, the more old-fashioned, homey look of a "domed" cake is more desirable.

Frosting Cakes

When frosting a cake, put a small dollop of frosting in the center of the plate to anchor the cake before putting the first layer on it. To keep the cake plate clean, insert four narrow strips of waxed paper under the edges of the layer, covering the rim of the plate. Then simply pull each one out from one end when you've finished.

Brush any loose crumbs from the cake layers, then fill and frost the layers as directed. Professionals and many other cake bakers like to first apply what is called a crumb coat, or skim coat, rather like spackling the cracks in a wall. Use a long metal spatula to spread a very thin layer of frosting or icing over the top and sides of the cake. It should be almost translucent; you aren't trying to cover the cake here. The skim coat "glues" any lurking crumbs to the cake so they won't mar the appearance of the finished cake, and it gives you an undercoat that will serve as a smooth base, making it easy to apply the rest of the frosting smoothly. Let the skim coat set (15 minutes in the refrigerator will usually do it), then frost the top and sides of the cake.

Cupcakes for Busy Moms

Bail out a busy, overstressed mom by baking these when it's her turn to provide the classroom treat. Two recipes follow, chocolate-frosted cupcakes and orange-flavored ones, both of which are perfect for Halloween, particularly when you turn the cream cheese frosting pumpkin-orange with food coloring. They're great for kids' parties as well, and you can let them decorate their very own cakes. Set out small bowls of colored sprinkles and so on, and tint the white frosting (page 62) other colors, if you like.

(If you don't have two large muffin pans, you can bake the cupcakes in batches; set the extra batter aside at room temperature while the first batch bakes.)

devil's food cupcakes

Makes 22 cupcakes

> 1¾ cups unbleached all-purpose flour
> ¼ cup plus 2 tablespoons unsweetened
>   cocoa powder (see page 12), sifted
> 1½ teaspoons baking soda
> ¼ teaspoon salt
> 10 tablespoons (1¼ sticks) unsalted butter,
>   at room temperature
> 1 cup granulated sugar
> ½ cup packed light brown sugar
> 2 large eggs
> 1½ teaspoons pure vanilla extract
> 1⅓ cups buttermilk

continued

Chocolate Frosting

4 ounces semisweet, bittersweet, or milk chocolate, coarsely chopped

8 tablespoons (1 stick) unsalted butter, at room temperature

2½ cups confectioners' sugar

4 to 6 tablespoons whole milk

1½ teaspoons pure vanilla extract

1. Put a rack in the middle of the oven and preheat the oven to 350°F. Line 22 muffin cups with foil or paper cupcake liners.

2. Whisk together the flour, cocoa powder, baking soda, and salt in a medium bowl.

3. In a large bowl, beat the butter and sugars with a mixer on medium speed until light and fluffy, 2 to 3 minutes. Scrape down the sides of the bowl. Add the eggs one at a time, beating well after each addition. Beat in the vanilla. On low speed, beat in the flour in three additions, alternating with the buttermilk in two additions and beating just until incorporated.

4. Spoon the batter into the muffin cups, filling each one about two-thirds full. Bake for 16 to 18 minutes, or until a toothpick inserted in the center of a cupcake comes out clean. Let the cupcakes cool in the pans for 10 minutes, then carefully transfer them to a wire rack to cool completely. *(The cupcakes can be baked up to 1 day ahead and stored in an airtight container at room temperature.)*

5. FOR THE FROSTING: Melt the chocolate in a metal bowl set over a saucepan of hot, not simmering, water (or melt it in the top of a double boiler), stirring until smooth. Remove the pan from the heat and let cool.

6. In a large bowl, beat the butter until creamy, about 30 seconds. Gradually beat in 1 cup of the confectioners' sugar. Beat in ¼ cup of the milk and the vanilla. Beat in the chocolate. Gradually beat in the remaining 1½ cups confectioners' sugar and continue to beat until the frosting reaches a spreadable consistency, adding up to 2 tablespoons more milk if necessary.

7. Spread the frosting generously over the cupcakes. Or transfer the frosting to a pastry bag fitted with a large star tip and pipe a generous swirl of frosting onto each cupcake. *(The frosted cupcakes can be stored in an airtight container for up to 2 days.)*

Fluffy White Frosting

Omit the chocolate in the frosting. Reduce the milk to 3 to 5 tablespoons and the vanilla to 1 teaspoon. Proceed as directed.

Matthew's birthday cake

When a good friend was super-busy and didn't have time to bake for her son's class party one year, I made this cake for her, and then she did the decorating.

1. Prepare the batter as directed (opposite) and scrape it into two buttered-and-floured 8-inch square cake pans. Bake for 30 to 35 minutes. Cool the cakes in the pans on a rack for 10 minutes; invert the cakes onto another rack, invert them again onto the first rack, and let cool completely.

2. Make a double recipe of the white frosting (page 62) and frost the cake. An easy way to decorate a kid's cake (especially for the artistically impaired, like me) is to use assorted cookie cutters—dinosaurs are good—to make imprints in the frosting around the sides and top of the cake, pressing gently to make an impression. Then outline the shapes using colored decorating gels from the supermarket. Use the same gels to handwrite any special greetings or the name of the recipient on top.

orange cupcakes with orange cream cheese frosting

Makes 24 cupcakes

Cupcakes aren't just for kids—grown-ups are especially fond of these orange-scented little cakes, which sport a luscious orange cream cheese frosting. They are also rather good topped with Chocolate Frosting (page 62).

3 cups unbleached all-purpose flour

1 tablespoon baking powder

½ teaspoon salt

14 tablespoons (1¾ sticks) unsalted
  butter, at room temperature

2 cups granulated sugar

4 large eggs

2 teaspoons pure orange extract

1 tablespoon grated orange zest

1½ cups whole milk

Orange Cream Cheese Frosting

One 8-ounce package cold cream cheese,
  cut into chunks

4 tablespoons unsalted butter,
  at room temperature

2 teaspoons grated orange zest

1 teaspoon pure orange extract

2 cups confectioners' sugar

1. Put a rack in the center of the oven and preheat the oven to 350°F. Line 24 muffin cups with foil or paper cupcake liners.

2. Whisk together the flour, baking powder, and salt in a medium bowl.

3. In a large bowl, beat the butter and sugar with an electric mixer on medium speed until light and fluffy, 2 to 3 minutes. Scrape down the sides of the bowl. Add the eggs one at a time, beating well after each addition. Beat in the orange extract and zest. On low speed, beat in the flour in three additions, alternating with the milk in two additions and beating just until incorporated.

4. Spoon the batter into the muffin cups, filling each cup about two-thirds full. Bake for 17 to 19 minutes, or until a toothpick inserted in the center of a cupcake comes out clean. Let the cupcakes cool in the pans for 10 minutes, then carefully transfer them to a wire rack to cool completely. (*The cupcakes can be baked up to 1 day ahead and stored in an airtight container at room temperature.*)

5. **FOR THE FROSTING:** In a large bowl, beat the cream cheese and butter with an electric mixer on medium speed until light and creamy. Beat in the orange zest and extract. On low speed, beat in the confectioners' sugar in two additions, beating until smooth.

6. Spread the frosting generously over the cupcakes. Or transfer the frosting to a pastry bag fitted with a large star tip and pipe a generous swirl of frosting onto each cupcake. *(The frosted cupcakes can be stored in an airtight container in the refrigerator for up to 2 days; bring to room temperature before serving.)*

coconut layer cake

Serves 10 to 12

The billowy white frosting for this cake is a variation on old-fashioned seven-minute icing (you beat it over heat for seven minutes). The first time I made the cake, I was immediately transported back to the special-occasion bakery cakes my family would buy when my grandmother came to visit. Like those cakes, this tall, stunning cake is perfect for a friend's wedding shower or anniversary celebration. For a real showstopper, turn this two-layer cake into a four-layer cake by slicing each layer horizontally in half (the frosting makes a generous amount, so there'll be plenty for layering). On the other hand, if you want an easy sheet cake (and one that's a bit easier to transport), see the variation.

$2^3/_4$ cups unbleached all-purpose flour

1 tablespoon baking powder

$1/_2$ teaspoon salt

14 tablespoons ($1^3/_4$ sticks) unsalted
   butter, at room temperature

2 cups sugar

4 large eggs

1 large egg yolk

2 teaspoons pure vanilla extract

$1^1/_3$ cups whole milk

Coconut Frosting

3 large egg whites, at room temperature

$2^1/_4$ cups sugar

$3/_8$ teaspoon cream of tartar

$7^1/_2$ tablespoons water

$2^1/_4$ teaspoons light corn syrup

$1/_2$ teaspoon pure vanilla extract

2 cups sweetened shredded coconut

1. Put a rack in the middle of the oven and preheat the oven to 350°F. Butter and flour two 9-inch round cake pans.

2. Whisk together the flour, baking powder, and salt in a medium bowl.

3. In a large bowl (use a stand mixer if you have one), beat the butter and sugar with an electric mixer on medium speed until light and fluffy, 2 to 3 minutes. Scrape down the sides of the bowl. Add the eggs and egg yolk one at a time, beating well after each addition. Beat in the vanilla. On low speed, beat in the flour mixture in three additions, alternating with the milk in two additions and beating just until incorporated.

4. Scrape the batter into the prepared pans and smooth the tops. Bake for 30 to 35 minutes, or until a toothpick inserted in the center of a cake comes out clean. Transfer the pans to a wire rack to cool for 10 minutes.

5. Run a knife around the edge of each pan to release the cake, invert the layers onto a rack, and then invert them again onto another rack to cool completely. *(The layers can be made up to 1 day ahead and kept, well wrapped, at room temperature.)*

6. **FOR THE FROSTING:** Combine the egg whites, sugar, cream of tartar, water, and corn syrup in a very large deep heatproof bowl. Using a hand-held mixer, beat on low speed just to combine. Set the bowl over a large pot of simmering water (the bottom of the bowl should not touch the water) and beat on medium speed, scraping down the sides of the bowl once or twice, for 3 minutes. Increase the speed to high and beat for 4 minutes longer, or until the frosting is thick and shiny and holds firm, but not stiff, peaks. Remove the bowl from the heat, add the vanilla, and beat on high speed until the frosting again holds firm peaks. Using a large rubber spatula, fold in ½ cup of the coconut. (The frosting should be used immediately.)

7. Put one cake layer upside down on a serving plate and spread a generous layer of frosting over the top. Place the second layer right side up on top and frost the top and sides of the cake generously with the remaining frosting. Scatter about ½ cup coconut evenly over the top of the cake, breaking up any clumps of coconut with your fingers, and press the remaining coconut onto the sides. *(The cake can be frosted up to 6 hours ahead and left at cool room temperature. Refrigerate any leftovers.)*

coconut sheet cake

Prepare the batter as directed, but scrape it into a buttered-and-floured 9-by-13-inch baking pan. Bake for about 40 minutes, and let the cake cool completely in the pan on a rack. For the frosting, use 2 large egg whites, 1½ cups sugar, ¼ teaspoon cream of tartar, 5 tablespoons water, 1½ teaspoons corn syrup, and ¼ teaspoon pure vanilla extract. Fold ½ cup of the coconut into the frosting. Frost the cake in the pan, then sprinkle the remaining 1½ cups coconut over the top of the frosted cake. Cut into squares to serve. (Makes 15 squares)

chocolate-frosted chocolate cake

Serves 8 to 10

When I set out to bake my favorite chocolate cake, I started with a lighter cake to balance this rich frosting. Although people liked it, I thought something was missing. Soon I realized that more chocolate (and more cocoa powder) was the answer. When I baked this version, a friend I asked to taste it said, "Now, *this* is a chocolate cake."

This is what I, like most chocolate lovers, consider chocolate layer cake, but for some, the "all-American" version is a golden cake with chocolate frosting. If you are one of those, frost the cake layers from the Coconut Layer Cake (page 66) with this fudgy frosting. Or, conversely, if you're making a cake for someone who loves both chocolate and coconut, frost the chocolate cake layers with the Coconut Frosting (page 66).

1½ cups unbleached all-purpose flour
⅔ cup Dutch-process cocoa powder
   (see page 12), sifted
1½ teaspoons baking powder
½ teaspoon baking soda
¼ teaspoon salt
12 tablespoons (1½ sticks) unsalted
   butter, at room temperature
1½ cups sugar
3 large eggs
1½ teaspoons pure vanilla extract
1 cup sour cream

Chocolate Fudge Frosting

10 ounces bittersweet or semisweet chocolate,
   coarsely chopped
1½ cups heavy cream
1½ tablespoons unsalted butter
1 teaspoon pure vanilla extract

1. Put a rack in the middle of the oven and preheat the oven to 350°F. Butter and flour two 9-inch round cake pans.

2. Whisk together the flour, cocoa, baking powder, baking soda, and salt in a medium bowl.

3. In a large bowl, beat the butter and sugar with an electric mixer on medium speed until light and fluffy, 2 to 3 minutes. Scrape down the sides of the bowl. Add the eggs one at a time, beating well after each addition. Beat in the vanilla. On low speed, beat in the flour mixture in three additions, alternating with the sour cream in two additions and beating just until incorporated.

4. Scrape the batter into the prepared pans and smooth the tops. Bake for 25 to 30 minutes, or until a toothpick inserted into the center of a cake comes out clean. Transfer the pans to a wire rack to cool for 10 minutes.

5. Run a knife around the edge of each pan to release the cake, then invert the layers onto another rack to cool completely. (*The cake layers can be made up to 1 day ahead and kept, well wrapped, at room temperature.*)

6. **FOR THE FROSTING:** Put the chocolate in a food processor and process until finely chopped. Combine the cream and butter in a medium heavy saucepan and bring to a boil. With the machine running, pour the cream into the processor and process just until the chocolate is completely melted, stopping once or twice to scrape down the sides of the bowl. Pour the mixture into a medium bowl and stir in the vanilla. Let cool to room temperature, then refrigerate, stirring occasionally with a rubber spatula, for 1 to 1½ hours, or until the frosting has thickened to a spreadable consistency.

7. Put one cake layer upside down on a serving plate. If you like, set aside about ½ cup of the frosting for garnishing the cake. Spread a thin layer of frosting over the top of the cake layer. Place the second layer right side up on top and frost the top and sides of the cake with the remaining frosting. If you reserved frosting for garnish, transfer it to a pastry bag fitted with a medium star tip and pipe a border of rosettes around the top of the cake. (*The cake can be stored, covered, at room temperature for up to 2 days.*)

old-fashioned spice cake with cream cheese frosting

Serves 10

This homey cake is actually best if its flavors are allowed to mellow overnight, so it's a great make-ahead dessert. Make the layer cake, or the even easier sheet cake variation, for a casual gathering with friends, kids included, or offer to bring it to your book group when the host is feeling overwhelmed.

2 cups unbleached all-purpose flour

2 teaspoons baking powder

½ teaspoon salt

1 teaspoon ground cinnamon

¼ teaspoon ground allspice

¼ teaspoon ground cloves

¼ teaspoon ground ginger

10 tablespoons (1¼ sticks) unsalted butter, at room temperature

1½ cups granulated sugar

3 large eggs

1 teaspoon pure vanilla extract

1 cup whole milk

Cream Cheese Frosting

10 ounces cold cream cheese, cut into chunks

6 tablespoons unsalted butter, at room temperature

1½ teaspoons pure vanilla extract

3 cups confectioners' sugar, sifted

1. Put a rack in the middle of the oven and preheat the oven to 350°F. Butter and flour two 9-inch round cake pans.

2. Whisk together the flour, baking powder, salt, cinnamon, allspice, cloves, and ginger in a medium bowl.

3. In a large bowl, beat the butter and sugar with an electric mixer on medium speed until light and fluffy, 2 to 3 minutes. Scrape down the sides of the bowl. Add the eggs one at a time, beating well after each addition. Beat in the vanilla. On low speed, beat in the flour in three additions, alternating with the milk in two additions and beating just until incorporated.

4. Scrape the batter into the prepared pans and smooth the top. Bake for 25 to 30 minutes, until a toothpick inserted in the center of a cake comes out clean but not dry. Transfer the pans to a wire rack to cool for 10 minutes.

5. Run a knife around the edge of each pan to release the cake, invert the layers onto a wire rack, and then invert them again onto another rack to cool completely. (*The layers can be made up to 1 day ahead and kept, well wrapped, at room temperature.*)

6. **FOR THE FROSTING**: Combine the cream cheese, butter, and vanilla in a large bowl and beat with an electric mixer on medium speed just until thoroughly blended. On low speed, beat in about one-third of the confectioners' sugar. Add the remaining confectioners' sugar in two additions, beating until blended and smooth.

7. Place one of the cake layers upside down on a serving plate and spread a generous layer of frosting (about ¼ inch thick) over the top. Place the second layer right side up on top and frost the top and sides of the cake with the remaining frosting: Swirl the frosting over the top, or use the back of a spoon to lift up "porcupine spikes" all over the top. (*The cake can be refrigerated, covered, for up to 2 days. Serve chilled or at room temperature.*)

 ### *easy spice sheet cake*

Prepare the batter as directed, but scrape it into a buttered-and-floured 9-by-13-inch baking pan. Increase the baking time to about 35 minutes and let the cake cool completely in the pan on a rack. For the frosting, use 7 ounces cream cheese, 4 tablespoons unsalted butter, 1 teaspoon pure vanilla extract, and 2 cups confectioners' sugar. Frost the cake in the pan, then cut the cake into squares. (Makes 15 squares)

ginger-peach upside-down cake

Serves 8

Upside-down cakes don't have to be made with pineapple and maraschino cherries: Ginger and peaches is one of my favorite combinations. Made with both crystallized and ground ginger, this can be dessert, a snack, or breakfast—it's great still warm from the oven. When berries are in season, make the fresh blueberry-lemon version, or try the completely nontraditional cherry–chocolate chip cake at any time of year. Vanilla ice cream complements any of these cakes.

Ginger-Peach Topping
4 tablespoons unsalted butter,
*   cut into 4 pieces*
¼ cup packed light brown sugar
2 cups canned peach slices in heavy
*   syrup, thoroughly drained*
2 tablespoons minced crystallized
*   ginger*

1⅓ cups unbleached all-purpose flour
1½ teaspoons baking powder
¼ teaspoon salt
½ teaspoon ground ginger
8 tablespoons (1 stick) unsalted butter,
*   at room temperature*
1 cup granulated sugar
2 large eggs
1½ teaspoons pure vanilla extract
½ cup whole milk

1. Put a rack in the middle of the oven and preheat the oven to 350°F.

2. **FOR THE TOPPING:** Melt the butter in a 9-inch round cake pan over low heat. Using a wooden spoon, stir in the brown sugar and cook, stirring, for about 3 minutes, or until the mixture is smooth and bubbling (it may look slightly grainy). Remove the pan from the heat.

3. Lay the peach slices on a double layer of paper towels and gently blot away excess moisture with another paper towel. Reserve 5 or 6 of the smaller slices for the center of the cake. Arrange the remaining slices side by side, without crowding, in a ring on the brown sugar mixture, about ¼ inch from the sides of the pan. Arrange the reserved slices in a pinwheel pattern in the center. Sprinkle the crystallized ginger evenly over the peaches. Set aside.

4. **FOR THE CAKE:** Whisk together the flour, baking powder, salt, and ground ginger in a small bowl.

5. In a large bowl, beat the butter and granulated sugar with an electric mixer on medium speed until light and fluffy, 2 to 3 minutes. Scrape down the sides of the bowl. Add the eggs one at a time, beating well after each addition. Beat in the vanilla. On low speed, beat in half the flour, then beat in the milk. Beat in the remaining flour just until incorporated.

6. Spoon the batter in large dollops over the peaches. Using a rubber spatula, carefully spread the batter over the peaches without disturbing them, covering them completely and making sure the batter reaches the edges of the pan (the peaches will be juicy).

7. Bake for 40 to 45 minutes, or until a toothpick inserted in the center of the cake comes out clean. Cool the cake in the pan on a wire rack for 3 minutes.

8. Run a knife around the edge of the pan to release the cake. Invert a wire rack over the cake, then invert the cake onto the rack and lift off the pan. (If any peach slices have stuck to the pan, replace them on top of the cake.) Set the rack on a baking sheet to catch any juices. Serve warm or at room temperature. (*The cooled cake can be stored, covered, at room temperature for up to 1 day.*)

blueberry-lemon upside-down cake

For the topping, increase the brown sugar to ⅔ cup. Substitute 2 cups fresh blueberries, rinsed and thoroughly drained, for the peaches. Omit the crystallized ginger and sprinkle 1½ teaspoons grated lemon zest over the blueberries in the pan. For the batter, omit the ground ginger and add 1½ teaspoons grated lemon zest along with the vanilla. Bake as directed.

cherry-chocolate chip upside-down cake

For the topping, increase the brown sugar to ½ cup. Substitute 2 cups canned dark sweet cherries in heavy syrup, thoroughly drained and patted dry, or 2 cups frozen dark sweet cherries (measured while still slightly frozen) for the peaches. Omit the crystallized ginger. For the batter, omit the ground ginger and fold in ⅔ cup mini chocolate chips at the end. Bake as directed.

two-ginger gingerbread

Makes 9 large or 16 smaller squares

Crystallized ginger is the secret to this delectable version of an old-fashioned favorite.
It's good served warm (I've delivered it hot out of the oven to friends who couldn't wait),
but letting it mellow at room temperature for a day, or even two, really intensifies its spicy
nature. Dark or "robust" molasses deepens the flavor, but you can use the lighter type
(sometimes labeled "original") if you'd like a slightly milder taste.

2 cups unbleached all-purpose flour

1 teaspoon baking soda

¼ teaspoon salt

2¼ teaspoons ground ginger

¾ teaspoon ground cinnamon

⅛ teaspoon ground cloves

8 tablespoons (1 stick) unsalted butter,
*   at room temperature*

¾ cup packed brown sugar

1 large egg

⅔ cup unsulphured molasses,
*   preferably dark*

⅔ cup very hot water

½ cup finely chopped crystallized ginger

Confectioners' sugar for dusting (optional)

1. Put a rack in the center of the oven and preheat the oven to 350°F. Butter and flour a 9-inch square cake pan.

2. Whisk together the flour, baking soda, salt, ground ginger, cinnamon, and cloves in a medium bowl.

3. In a large bowl (use a stand mixer if you have one), beat the butter and brown sugar with an electric mixer on medium speed until light and fluffy, 2 to 3 minutes. Scrape down the sides of the bowl. Beat in the egg until well blended. Beat in the molasses and hot water and then the crystallized ginger. On low speed, beat in the flour in two additions, beating just until incorporated (the batter will be stiff).

4. Scrape the batter into the prepared pan and smooth the top. Bake for 40 to 45 minutes, or until a toothpick inserted in the center of the cake comes out clean. Transfer the pan to a rack to cool for 20 minutes, then cut the cake into squares and serve warm. Or cool the cake completely in the pan and cover tightly until ready to serve, then dust the cake with confectioners' sugar, if you wish, and cut it into squares. (*The gingerbread can be stored at room temperature for up to 3 days.*)

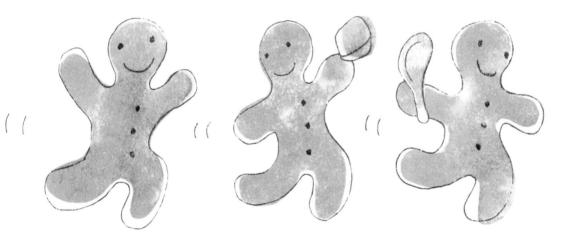

chocolate-raspberry squares

Makes 24 squares

These squares actually started out as a brownie-type bar, but I somehow made them with twice as much butter as I'd meant to use. Once I tasted them, however, I decided these light, cakelike squares were even better than my original idea. Flavored with raspberry jam, they are topped with a rich chocolate frosting laced with black raspberry liqueur. If you're pressed for time or feeling less inclined to indulge, you can skip the frosting and just sift confectioners' sugar over the tops of the squares.

3 ounces bittersweet chocolate,
  coarsely chopped
1 cup unbleached all-purpose flour
¼ teaspoon salt
½ pound (2 sticks) unsalted butter,
  at room temperature
1¼ cups sugar
3 large eggs
Scant ¼ cup seedless raspberry jam
1 teaspoon pure vanilla extract

Rich Chocolate Frosting

4 ounces bittersweet or semisweet chocolate,
  finely chopped
½ cup heavy cream
1 tablespoon Chambord (black raspberry
  liqueur) or 1 teaspoon pure vanilla extract

1. Put a rack in the center of the oven and preheat the oven to 350°F. Lightly grease a 9-by-13-inch baking pan.

2. Melt the chocolate in a heatproof bowl set over a saucepan of hot, not simmering, water (or melt it in a double boiler), stirring until smooth. Remove from the heat and set aside.

3. Whisk together the flour and salt in a medium bowl.

4. In a large bowl, beat the butter and sugar with an electric mixer on medium speed until light and fluffy, 2 to 3 minutes. Scrape down the sides of the bowl. Add the eggs one at a time, beating well after each addition. Add the jam, beating until well blended. Beat in the melted chocolate, then beat in the vanilla. On low speed, beat in the flour in two additions, beating just until incorporated.

5. Scrape the batter into the prepared pan and smooth the top. Bake for 25 to 30 minutes, or until a toothpick inserted in the center of the cake comes out clean but not dry. Transfer the pan to a wire rack to cool completely. *(The cake can be made up to 1 day ahead and kept, tightly covered, at room temperature.)*

6. **MEANWHILE, FOR THE FROSTING:** Put the chocolate in a medium bowl. In a small saucepan, bring the cream to a boil. Pour the cream over the chocolate and let stand for 30 seconds, then whisk gently until completely smooth. Whisk in the Chambord. Let the mixture cool to room temperature, then refrigerate just until spreadable, 30 minutes to 1 hour. *(The frosting can be refrigerated, covered, for up to 2 days. Bring to room temperature and stir until smooth before using.)*

7. Using a long metal spatula, spread the frosting evenly over the top of the cake. Cut the cake into 24 squares. Serve at room temperature or just slightly chilled. *(The squares can be stored in an airtight container at room temperature for up to 2 days or refrigerated for up to 4 days; let stand at room temperature to soften the frosting before serving.)*

little lemon loaves

Makes 6 small loaves

A friend now bakes these small loaf cakes as thank-you treats on teacher appreciation day. The loaves keep well, so you might want to make them part of your holiday baking and tuck one or two into the gift boxes you are shipping. Moist and buttery, they are delicious with a dusting of confectioners' sugar, but the easy glaze adds even more lemon flavor. Disposable (and inexpensive) foil mini loaf pans are available at many supermarkets and in housewares departments, in packages of five or eight.

2¼ cups unbleached all-purpose flour

1¼ teaspoons baking powder

½ teaspoon baking soda

½ teaspoon salt

½ pound (2 sticks) unsalted butter,
   at room temperature

2¼ cups sugar

4 large eggs

2 teaspoons packed grated lemon zest

2 teaspoons pure lemon extract

One 16-ounce container sour cream

Lemony Glaze (optional)

¾ cup confectioners' sugar, sifted

1 to 2 tablespoons fresh lemon juice

1. Put a rack in the middle of the oven and preheat the oven to 350°F. Butter and flour six 5¾-by-3-by-2-inch loaf pans.

2. Whisk together the flour, baking powder, baking soda, and salt in a medium bowl.

3. In a large bowl, beat the butter and sugar with an electric mixer on medium speed until light and fluffy, 2 to 3 minutes. Scrape down the sides of the bowl. Add the eggs one at a time, beating well after each addition. Beat in the lemon zest and the lemon extract. On low speed, beat in the flour mixture in three additions, alternating with the sour cream in two additions and beating just until incorporated.

4. Scrape the batter into the prepared pans and smooth the tops. Bake for 32 to 34 minutes, or until a toothpick inserted in the center of a cake comes out with just a few moist crumbs clinging to it. Transfer the pans to a rack to cool for 10 minutes.

5. Run a knife around the edges of each pan to release the cake, invert the cakes onto another rack, and then turn the cakes right side up to cool completely.

6. **FOR THE OPTIONAL GLAZE:** Put the rack of cakes on a baking sheet. Whisk together the confectioners' sugar and 1 tablespoon lemon juice in a small bowl, then whisk in enough additional lemon juice, a few drops at a time, to make a smooth glaze. Spoon about 1 tablespoon glaze down the center of the top of each cake, letting some of the glaze drip down the sides. Let stand until the glaze has set. *(The cakes, glazed or unglazed, can be stored, well wrapped or in an airtight container, for up to 5 days.)*

4

a tartlet for you, a tartlet for me

DESPITE THE WIDESPREAD "fear of pastry" that affects even some experienced cooks, making a piecrust is really quite easy. And making a tart shell is easier still, even though tarts may seem more professional or sophisticated than pies. So I've included several tart recipes here, along with my favorite pies. You'll also find recipes for three different individual tartlets. There's something about having a special little dessert that's all your own—and these little tarts are easy to transport, making them perfect for giving away. Even better, because each recipe makes four tartlets, you can keep one, or perhaps two, for yourself.

Both of the doughs used for these recipes, a flaky pie dough and a crisp confectioners' sugar tart dough, are made in the food processor, so there's no need to worry about working the butter into the flour with your fingertips or with one of those old-fashioned pastry blenders. It is important not to overwork any dough, or it may become tough, but that just means stopping the processor sooner rather than later (there are detailed instructions in the recipes). Tart dough is by its very nature less intimidating in this regard: A tart shell is not supposed to be flaky, as piecrust is; instead, it is crisp and/or crumbly. Tart dough is really more like a cookie dough—so the butter should be more evenly incorporated than in a pie dough (where the still-visible bits of butter in the dough make the dough flaky as they melt during baking). Also, because the tart shells are prebaked, you can make them in advance, whenever you have the time, and then there they are, ready to be filled. Prebaking the shell also means you don't have to worry about the problem of soggy bottom crusts, which can be a concern with a double-crust pie (as it happens, all the pies in this chapter use prebaked crusts too, so it's not an issue here).

If you feel at all intimidated by the idea of rolling out dough, you can roll out either of these doughs between sheets of parchment or waxed paper. (I usually just roll mine out on a lightly floured countertop; I have a marble pastry slab, but I didn't use it for any of these recipes.) Roll from the center of the dough outward, changing the angle with each roll so you work all around the circle of dough. You do want to be careful not to roll over the edges of the dough, or they could become too thin. Then either fold the round of dough in half or into quarters, lift it into the pie or tart pan, and unfold it, or roll it up loosely on the rolling pin and unroll it into the pan. Or, if you rolled out the dough between sheets of paper, lift off the top sheet, carefully invert the dough into the pan, peel off the second sheet, and fit the dough into the pan.

All of the pies in this chapter are made in a nine-inch glass pie plate. For the tarts, you will need a nine-inch fluted tart pan with a removable bottom; these pans are now widely available, even in many supermarkets. For the tartlets, I happen to have small fluted pans from the days when I used to make restaurant desserts in my (tiny) kitchen, but the aluminum foil pans you can find in almost any supermarket work fine. About $4\frac{1}{2}$ inches across at the top and $1\frac{1}{4}$ inches high, they look like individual pie pans but are usually labeled tart pans. I recommend doubling these lightweight pans when you use them so you avoid the possibility of burning the bottom of the crust. As the recipes in this chapter make four tartlets, and the pans come in sets of eight, that's easily done.

white chocolate tartlets topped with strawberries

Makes 4 tartlets

These white chocolate tarts are especially good when strawberries are at the height of season. They are also extremely easy to play with to create your own: Ripe raspberries or other berries are obvious alternatives for the strawberries, and if white chocolate just won't do, substituting bittersweet or semisweet chocolate will yield an equally rich dark chocolate filling.

White Chocolate Filling
2½ ounces white chocolate
   (see page 12), finely chopped
½ cup heavy cream

Sweet Tartlet Shells (page 90), baked and cooled
About 1½ cups very small strawberries, rinsed,
   dried, and hulled, or 1½ cups halved or
   quartered larger strawberries

1. **FOR THE FILLING:** Put the white chocolate in a small bowl. Bring the cream to a boil in a small saucepan. Pour the cream over the white chocolate and let stand for 30 seconds, then whisk gently until the white chocolate is melted and smooth. Let the mixture cool to room temperature, then refrigerate, stirring occasionally with a rubber spatula, until it is very cold but not set, 45 minutes to 1 hour.

2. With an electric mixer, beat the white chocolate mixture on low speed just until it holds soft peaks. Spoon the mixture into the baked tartlet shells and smooth the tops. If the filling is very soft, refrigerate the tartlets for about 30 minutes to set and firm the filling slightly.

3. Arrange or scatter the strawberries on the tops of the tartlets. Refrigerate the tartlets until ready to serve. *(The tartlets can be refrigerated for up to 1 day.)*

berry tartlets with sweet mascarpone

Makes 4 tartlets

Mascarpone is a rich, creamy Italian cheese, available in tubs in many supermarkets as well as in gourmet markets. Sweetened with a little sugar, mascarpone is delectable, but you could also add ¼ to ½ teaspoon of vanilla extract or a splash of liqueur. Chambord (black raspberry) pairs nicely with raspberries and blackberries, Grand Marnier with blueberries. Raspberries and blackberries are striking together, but whatever berries are in season—or even just one type—will be sensational as well.

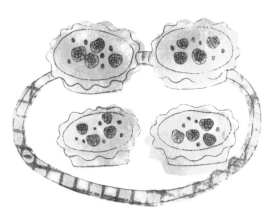

Mascarpone Filling

1 cup mascarpone (about 8 ounces)

2 tablespoons superfine sugar

Sweet Tartlet Shells (page 90),
*   baked and cooled*
About 1⅓ cups mixed berries,
*   such as raspberries, blackberries,*
*   marionberries, and/or blueberries*
Confectioners' sugar for dusting (optional)

1. **FOR THE FILLING:** Put the mascarpone in a medium bowl and stir it with a spoon or rubber spatula to loosen it slightly. Stir in the sugar.

2. Spoon the filling into the baked tartlet shells and smooth the tops. Arrange the berries on top of the filling. Refrigerate the tartlets until ready to serve. (*The tartlets can be made up to 1 day ahead.*) Just before serving, dust the tartlets with confectioners' sugar, if you like.

lemon cream cheese tartlets

Makes 4 tartlets

Top these lemony tarts with whatever suits your fancy—a few slivers of lemon zest (remove a strip or two of zest with a vegetable peeler, then cut into slivers with a sharp knife), candied lemon peel cut into strips or dice, or raspberries or other fresh berries.

Lemon Cream Cheese Filling

One 3-ounce package cream cheese,
   cut into chunks

¼ cup plus 2 tablespoons superfine sugar

1 teaspoon grated lemon zest

1 tablespoon fresh lemon juice

⅓ cup heavy cream

Sweet Tartlet Shells (page 90),
   baked and cooled

1. FOR THE FILLING: In a medium bowl, beat the cream cheese with an electric mixer on medium speed until light and creamy. Add the sugar, lemon zest, and lemon juice and beat until light and fluffy.

2. In a small bowl, beat (no need to wash the beaters) the cream until it holds soft peaks. Using a rubber spatula, fold a few spoonfuls of cream into the cream cheese mixture to lighten it, then fold in the remaining cream.

3. Spoon the filling into the baked tartlet shells, mounding it slightly in the center. Refrigerate the tartlets for at least 30 minutes. *(The tartlets can be refrigerated for up to 1 day.)*

super-easy lemon tart

Serves 8

This lovely tart is a good winter dessert, but in summer it's a knockout garnished with raspberries or other fresh berries. Cover the lemon filling completely with berries (you will need about 3 cups, or 1½ pints), then finish the tart with a dusting of confectioners' sugar. Lemon curd is the rather inelegant name for a delicious custardy spread or filling (the British are particularly fond of it at teatime), and excellent jarred lemon curd is available in most supermarkets, making it a great shortcut ingredient to keep on hand.

Lemon Filling

One 11-ounce jar high-quality
  lemon curd

1 cup heavy cream

2 tablespoons sugar

Sweet Tart Shell (page 90),
  baked and cooled

1. **FOR THE FILLING:** Put ⅓ cup of the lemon curd in a small bowl, cover, and set aside at room temperature. Using a rubber spatula, spread the remaining lemon curd evenly over the bottom of the baked tart shell. Refrigerate for 30 minutes, or until the lemon curd is chilled.

2. Beat the cream and sugar in a large bowl with an electric mixer until the cream holds firm peaks. Gently but thoroughly fold in the reserved lemon curd. (If the cream deflates too much, you can beat it gently just until it holds firm peaks again, but be careful not to overbeat it.)

3. Spoon the lemon cream into the tart shell and spread it gently over the lemon curd layer. Refrigerate the tart for at least 2 hours. *(The tart can be refrigerated for up to 6 hours.)*

blueberry-raspberry tart

Serves 8

This glistening summer tart looks like something from a sophisticated Parisian pastry shop, but it's amazingly easy to make. Because only some of the berries are cooked—just enough to hold the filling together—it is extraordinarily fresh tasting. You can vary the berries depending on what looks best at the farmers' market or supermarket, substituting blackberries or halved or quartered strawberries for the raspberries or even using all blueberries.

Berry Filling

1 pint fresh blueberries

1½ tablespoons cornstarch

¼ cup plus 2 tablespoons water

⅔ cup sugar

Generous pinch of salt

½ pint fresh raspberries, preferably small to medium size

Sweet Tart Shell (page 90), baked and cooled

1. **FOR THE FILLING**: Process ¾ cup of the blueberries in a food processor until finely chopped and juicy but not pureed; stop once or twice to scrape down the sides of the bowl. Put the remaining blueberries in a large bowl and set aside.

2. Combine the cornstarch and 2 tablespoons of the water in a small cup, stirring until smooth. Combine the remaining ¼ cup water, the sugar, and salt in a medium saucepan. Add the chopped blueberries and bring to a boil over medium heat, stirring occasionally. Stir the cornstarch mixture and add it to the pan, stirring constantly. Bring back to a boil, stirring constantly, and boil, stirring, for 1 minute.

3. Pour the hot blueberry mixture over the berries in the bowl and stir gently with a rubber spatula until they are evenly coated. Gently fold in the raspberries until coated. Pour the mixture into the tart shell, making sure to distribute the raspberries fairly evenly, and smooth the top (shake the tart pan gently if necessary to level the filling). Refrigerate the tart for at least 2 hours, or until the filling is set. *(The tart can be refrigerated for up to 8 hours. Cover it loosely once the filling is set.)*

chocolate-caramel tart

Serves 8

Chocolate and caramel are an unbeatable pair, and one of my favorite ways to combine them is by topping a thin layer of creamy chocolate ganache with a whipped caramel cream for a deceptively simple, rich tart. Garnish it with chocolate curls or shavings if you like.

Creamy Chocolate Filling	**Caramel Filling**
3½ ounces chocolate, coarsely chopped	¼ cup sugar
¾ cup heavy cream	2 tablespoons water
	1½ cups heavy cream
Sweet Tart Shell (page 90), baked and cooled	

1. FOR THE CHOCOLATE FILLING: Put the chocolate in a food processor and process until finely chopped. Bring the cream to a boil in a small saucepan. With the machine running, pour the hot cream into the processor and process just until the chocolate is completely melted, stopping to scrape down the sides of the bowl once or twice.

2. Pour the filling into the baked tart shell and refrigerate until the filling is chilled and set, at least 1½ hours. *(The tart can be made to this point up to 1 day ahead; cover tightly with plastic wrap.)*

3. MEANWHILE, FOR THE CARAMEL FILLING: Combine the sugar and water in a medium heavy saucepan and bring to a boil over medium-high heat, stirring occasionally to dissolve the sugar. Wash down the sides of the pan with a wet pastry brush to remove any sugar crystals (which could cause the caramel to crystallize). Boil, without stirring, until the caramel is a golden amber, 5 to 8 minutes; once the caramel starts to darken in color, swirl the pan occasionally so the caramel cooks evenly.

4. Immediately remove the pan from the heat and, standing back, slowly add the cream (the mixture will bubble up). Return the pan to low heat and cook, stirring occasionally with a wooden spoon, until the caramel dissolves. Pour the caramel cream into a large bowl and let cool to room temperature, then refrigerate, covered, until very cold, at least 2 hours.

5. Beat the caramel cream with an electric mixer just until it is beginning to hold firm peaks. Scrape the filling onto the chilled tart and smooth the top. Refrigerate the tart for at least 2 hours. *(The tart can be refrigerated for up to 8 hours.)*

whipped chocolate tart

Serves 8

Unlike chocolate cream pie, which is basically chocolate pudding in a piecrust, this tart uses the rich mixture of cream and chocolate known as ganache. It is whipped once it's been chilled, which lightens both the color and the texture—the filling literally melts in your mouth. Instead of flavoring it with the vanilla, you could use 1 to 2 tablespoons of Grand Marnier, Kahlúa, or another liqueur.

Whipped Chocolate Filling

7 ounces bittersweet or semisweet chocolate,
  coarsely chopped
1 1/2 cups heavy cream
1/2 teaspoon pure vanilla extract

Sweet Tart Shell (page 90), baked and cooled

Garnish (optional)

1/2 cup heavy cream
1 to 2 teaspoons sugar

1. FOR THE FILLING: Put the chocolate in a food processor and process until finely chopped. Bring the cream to a boil in a medium saucepan. With the machine running, add the hot cream to the processor and process until the chocolate is completely melted, about 30 seconds, stopping once or twice to scrape down the sides of the bowl. Transfer the chocolate mixture to a medium bowl and stir in the vanilla. Let the filling cool to room temperature, then refrigerate, stirring occasionally with a rubber spatula, until it is very cold but not set, 1 to 1 3/4 hours.

2. With an electric mixer, beat the chocolate mixture on low speed just until it lightens in color and holds soft peaks. Scrape the mixture into the baked tart shell and smooth the top. Refrigerate the tart until the filling is set, at least 2 hours. *(The tart can be refrigerated for up to 1 day.)*

3. Up to 1 hour before serving, garnish the tart, if you like: Combine the cream and sugar in a small bowl and beat with an electric mixer until the cream just holds stiff peaks. Scrape the cream into a pastry bag fitted with a large star tip and pipe rosettes around the edge of the pie or spoon dollops of cream all around the pie.

sweet tart shell (or tartlet shells)

Makes one 9-inch tart shell or four 4-inch tartlet shells

The confectioners' sugar gives this cookielike pastry a great texture. The dough is easy to work with, and is very forgiving—if it tears at any point as you are working with it, simply patch it with a scrap of dough. The tart shell (or shells) can be baked up to a day in advance (cover tightly with plastic wrap once cooled). And the recipe is easily doubled (freeze half the dough, if you like, ready to roll out at a later date).

1¼ cups unbleached all-purpose flour
¼ cup confectioners' sugar
Generous pinch of salt
6 tablespoons unsalted butter, cut into ½-inch cubes and chilled
2 to 3 tablespoons ice water

1. Combine the flour, confectioners' sugar, and salt in a food processor and pulse 3 or 4 times to blend. Scatter the butter over the flour and pulse 10 to 15 times, until the mixture resembles coarse meal. Add 2 tablespoons ice water and pulse just until the dough starts to come together, adding up to 1 more tablespoon water, a teaspoon at a time, if necessary.

2. Turn the dough out onto a work surface. **FOR A TART SHELL**, shape it into a 5-inch disk and wrap it in plastic wrap. **FOR TARTLET SHELLS**, divide the dough into quarters, shape each piece into a 3½- to 4-inch disk, and wrap each disk in plastic wrap. Refrigerate the dough for at least 30 minutes. *(The dough can be refrigerated for up to 1 day or frozen, well wrapped, for up to 1 month; thaw in the refrigerator. If necessary, let the dough stand briefly at room temperature to soften slightly before rolling it out.)*

3. **FOR A TART SHELL**, on a lightly floured surface, roll out the dough to a 12-inch round. Fold the dough in half or into quarters and transfer it to a fluted 9-inch tart pan with a removable bottom. Unfold the dough and carefully fit it into the pan, pressing it gently against the sides without stretching it. Roll the rolling pin across the top of the pan to remove the excess dough. Refrigerate for 30 minutes to 1 hour. **FOR TARTLET SHELLS**, roll each piece into a 6½-inch round and fit it into a 4-inch fluted tart pan with a removable bottom or a 4- to 4½-inch foil tart pan (see Note). If using fluted tart pans, roll the rolling pin across the top of each pan to remove excess dough; if using foil pans, use a sharp knife to trim the dough even with the top of the pans. Set each foil pan in another pan. Refrigerate for 30 minutes to 1 hour.

4. Put a rack in the lower third of the oven and preheat the oven to 375°F.

5. Line the tart (or tartlet) shell with foil and fill it with dried beans, rice, or pie weights. Bake for 18 minutes. Carefully remove the foil and weights and bake for 6 to 8 minutes longer, or until golden brown. Transfer the pan(s) to a rack to cool completely.

NOTE: Individual foil tart pans are available, in packages of eight, in many supermarkets. They look like small pie pans but are usually labeled tart pans. Doubling up the pans helps prevent the bottom of the crust from burning.

cranberry and dried cherry pie

Serves 8 to 10

With its gorgeous red filling, this is, of course, perfect for the winter holidays—offer to bring it for the Thanksgiving gathering or take it to a friend's Christmas Eve open house. To make it even more festive, you could cut leaves or cherries or other shapes from the scraps of dough, using tiny cutters or a paring knife, and bake them with the pie shell on a small baking sheet until golden brown. Then arrange the shapes decoratively on top of the cooled pie.

Cranberry-Cherry Filling

1½ tablespoons cornstarch

¼ cup plus 2 tablespoons
    orange juice

1¼ cups sugar

2½ cups fresh or frozen
    (not thawed) cranberries,
    picked over

1 cup (about 5 ounces) dried cherries

Flaky Pie Shell (page 98),
    baked and cooled

1. **FOR THE FILLING:** Combine the cornstarch and 2 tablespoons of the orange juice in a small cup and stir until smooth.

2. Combine the remaining ¼ cup orange juice and the sugar in a large heavy saucepan and cook over medium heat, stirring, until the sugar is dissolved. Stir in the cranberries and dried cherries, increase the heat to medium high, and bring to a boil, stirring occasionally. Stir the cornstarch mixture, then stir it into the cranberries. Bring the mixture back to a boil, stirring frequently, and cook, stirring, until the cooking juices are clear and slightly thickened, 1 to 2 minutes. Transfer the mixture to a large bowl and let cool to room temperature.

3. Scrape the filling into the pie shell and refrigerate the pie for at least 4 hours, or until the filling is set. *(The pie can be refrigerated for up to 1 day; cover it loosely once the filling is set.)*

mocha silk pie

Serves 8

If you have a stand mixer, you'll want to use it for this—it's essential to beat the filling for the amount of time specified in order for it to achieve its silky-smooth texture. If you're making the pie for someone who isn't a big coffee lover, just omit the espresso powder, for a wonderful chocolate filling. This rich pie doesn't really need any garnish, but there's no reason you couldn't finish it with rosettes or dollops of whipped cream and a few chocolate-covered coffee beans.

Mocha Filling

*1 teaspoon instant espresso coffee powder
    (such as Medaglia d'Oro) or 2 teaspoons
    instant coffee granules*

1½ teaspoons pure vanilla extract

*12 tablespoons (1½ sticks) unsalted butter,
    at room temperature*

¾ cup superfine sugar

*3 ounces semisweet chocolate,
    melted and cooled*

3 large eggs, at room temperature

Flaky Pie Shell (page 98), baked and cooled

1. **FOR THE FILLING:** Combine the espresso powder and vanilla in a small cup and stir to dissolve the espresso. Set aside.

2. In a large bowl (preferably the bowl of a stand mixer), beat the butter and sugar on medium speed until light and fluffy, 2 to 3 minutes. Scrape down the sides of the bowl. Beat in the coffee mixture, then beat in the melted chocolate. Add the eggs one at a time, beating for a full 3 minutes after each addition.

3. Scrape the filling into the pie shell and smooth the top. Refrigerate the pie for at least 4 hours, or until set. (*The pie can be refrigerated for up to 1 day.*)

peanut butter pie with a chocolate cookie crust

Serves 10

Peanut butter pie is a guilty pleasure that is impossible to resist. The classic filling for this all-American dessert includes cream cheese, which adds to its richness; it also gives the filling a slight tang, which some people love, but some—as I learned—don't. So I also make a somewhat lighter (though no less rich) variation without cream cheese, and I've included both versions here.

Either one takes only minutes to put together, but the filling and chocolate topping do need time to chill. In fact, the filling tastes more peanut buttery if you refrigerate it overnight. Depending on your schedule or the occasion, you can finish either version with the chocolate topping or simply scatter chocolate curls or shavings over the top.

Chocolate Cookie Crust

1½ cups chocolate wafer cookie crumbs
　　(from about 25 cookies, such as
　　Nabisco Famous Wafers)
5 tablespoons unsalted butter, melted

Peanut Butter Filling

1 cup smooth peanut butter
　　(not "natural style")
6 ounces cream cheese, cut into chunks
1 cup confectioners' sugar
1 cup heavy cream
1½ teaspoons pure
　　vanilla extract

Chocolate Ganache Topping

5 ounces bittersweet or semisweet chocolate,
　　coarsely chopped
½ cup heavy cream

1. **FOR THE CRUST:** Combine the cookie crumbs and melted butter in a medium bowl, stirring until the crumbs are evenly moistened. Press the mixture firmly and evenly over the bottom and up the sides of a 9-inch pie pan (use a flat-bottomed drinking glass to press the crumbs over the bottom of the shell). Refrigerate for 30 minutes to set the crust.

2. **FOR THE FILLING:** In a large bowl, beat the peanut butter, cream cheese, and confectioners' sugar with an electric mixer on medium speed until smooth and creamy.

3. In a medium bowl, beat (no need to wash the beaters) the cream and vanilla until the cream holds soft peaks. Using a rubber spatula, stir about ½ cup of the whipped cream into the peanut butter mixture to lighten it, then fold in the remaining cream in two batches.

4. Scrape the filling into the chilled piecrust, mounding it slightly in the center. Refrigerate for at least 1 hour, or until the filling is cold.

5. **FOR THE TOPPING:** Put the chocolate in a food processor and process until finely chopped. Bring the cream to a boil in a small saucepan. With the machine running, pour the hot cream into the processor and process just until the chocolate is completely melted, stopping to scrape down the sides of the bowl once or twice. Pour the chocolate mixture into a 2-cup glass measure or a small bowl with a pour spout and let cool to room temperature (the topping should still be fluid enough to pour).

6. Pour the topping evenly over the top of the chilled pie, spreading it evenly with a long metal spatula. Refrigerate the pie for at least 4 hours. *(The pie can be refrigerated for up to 1 day.)*

7. Use a hot knife (dipped into hot water and wiped dry between each slice) to cut the pie into wedges.

whipped cream peanut butter pie

Prepare and chill the crust as directed. For the filling, use ¾ cup peanut butter, ¾ cup confectioners' sugar, 1½ cups heavy cream, and 1 teaspoon pure vanilla extract; omit the cream cheese. In a large bowl, combine the peanut butter and ¼ cup of the confectioners' sugar and beat until blended. In a medium bowl, combine the cream, the remaining ½ cup confectioners' sugar, and the vanilla and beat (no need to wash the beaters) until the cream holds firm peaks. Stir about ½ cup of the whipped cream into the peanut butter to lighten it, then gently but thoroughly fold in the remaining cream; do not overmix. Scrape the filling into the pie shell and refrigerate the pie for at least 2 hours. Just before serving, garnish the pie with chocolate curls or shavings.

apple and brown butter crostata

Serves 6

A *crostata* is a rustic free-form Italian tart; a *galette* is the French version. This one is an easier version of the labor-intensive individual galettes I used to make back in my pastry chef days. Here the brown butter gives the filling a subtle nutty flavor that complements crisp Granny Smith apples. (You can also use Golden Delicious apples, which are less tart.) This is best the day it is made—it's great warm from the oven, or you can rewarm it before serving—but both the filling and the dough can be made in advance, and the crostata is easy to put together at the last minute.

Brown Butter Filling

4 tablespoons unsalted butter

½ vanilla bean, split, or ½ teaspoon
   pure vanilla extract

1 large egg

¼ cup plus 2 tablespoons sugar

Pinch of salt

3½ tablespoons unbleached
   all-purpose flour

Dough for Flaky Pie Shell (page 98)

2 large or 3 small Granny Smith or
   Golden Delicious apples

½ lemon

2 tablespoons sugar

1 tablespoon unsalted butter, melted

1. **FOR THE FILLING:** Combine the butter and vanilla bean, if using (not the extract), in a small heavy saucepan and cook over medium heat until the butter is golden brown and has a nutty aroma, about 10 minutes; there will be brown specks in the bottom of the pan.

2. Meanwhile, whisk the egg and sugar in a small bowl until well blended. Whisk in the salt, then add the flour and whisk until smooth.

3. Remove the vanilla bean from the butter and discard. Whisking constantly, slowly add the butter to the egg yolk mixture (leave any very dark brown specks—these are the milk solids—in the bottom of the pan). Whisk in the vanilla extract, if using. Let cool, then cover the filling and refrigerate for at least 1 hour. *(The filling can be made up to 2 days ahead.)*

4. Put a rack in the lower third of the oven and preheat the oven to 425°F. Line a large heavy baking sheet with foil or parchment paper.

5. On a lightly floured surface, roll out the dough to a rough 14-inch round. Roll the dough up on the rolling pin and transfer to the baking sheet, letting the dough hang over the sides of the baking sheet. Refrigerate the dough while you prepare the apples.

6. Peel, halve, and core the apples. Rub the apple halves with the lemon half to prevent them from darkening. Cut each apple half crosswise into ⅛-inch-thick slices, transfer to a bowl, and toss with a few drops of lemon juice.

7. Using a metal spatula, spread the filling evenly over the dough, leaving a 2-inch border all around. Scatter the apple slices evenly over the filling (it's OK if some of the slices break). Sprinkle the sugar over the apples and drizzle them with the melted butter. Fold the edges of the dough over the apples, pleating the dough as necessary (don't worry if there are a few tears in the dough, but pinch closed any gaps at the bottom so the filling doesn't leak out).

8. Bake the crostata for 20 minutes. Reduce the heat to 375°F and bake for 18 to 20 minutes longer, or until the crust is a deep golden brown. Transfer the pan to a rack to cool and serve warm or at room temperature. *(Once cooled, the crostata can be kept at room temperature, loosely covered, for up to 8 hours.)*

flaky pie shell

Makes one 9-inch pie shell

Your pie shell will have the richest flavor if you use all butter, but a combination of butter and a little vegetable shortening (see the variation) will result in a flakier crust. In either case, do not overwork the dough. The secret of a flaky crust *is,* as they say, a light hand. The dough can be refrigerated overnight or frozen for up to 1 month, and the pie shell can be baked up to a day ahead (cover tightly with plastic wrap once cooled).

> $1\frac{1}{3}$ cups unbleached all-purpose flour
>
> 2 tablespoons sugar
>
> $\frac{1}{4}$ teaspoon salt
>
> 8 tablespoons (1 stick) unsalted butter,
>   cut into $\frac{1}{2}$-inch cubes and chilled
>
> 2 to 3 tablespoons ice water

1. Combine the flour, sugar, and salt in a food processor and pulse to blend. Scatter the butter over the flour and pulse 10 to 15 times, or until the mixture resembles coarse meal, with some pea-sized lumps of butter. Add 2 tablespoons ice water and pulse briefly to incorporate. Pinch a bit of dough between your fingertips—if it doesn't hold together, add just enough water, 1 teaspoon at a time, for it to hold together when pinched but still be crumbly. Do not overprocess or the crust will not be flaky.

2. Turn the crumbly mixture out onto a large sheet of plastic wrap or into a medium bowl and knead briefly, just until the dough comes together. Shape the dough into a disk, wrap it in plastic wrap, and refrigerate it for at least 30 minutes before rolling it out. *(The dough can be refrigerated for up to 1 day or frozen, well wrapped, for up to 1 month; thaw in the refrigerator. If necessary, let the dough stand briefly at room temperature to soften slightly before rolling it out.)*

3. On a lightly floured surface, roll out the dough to a 12½-inch round. Fit it into a 9-inch pie pan. Trim the edges of the dough, leaving a ½-inch overhang. Fold the excess dough under itself and flute the edge to form a decorative border. Refrigerate the pie shell for 30 minutes to 1 hour.

4. To prebake the pie shell, put a rack in the lower third of the oven and preheat the oven to 375°F.

5. Line the pie shell with aluminum foil and fill it with dried beans, rice, or pie weights. Bake for 15 minutes. Remove the foil and weights and bake for 8 to 10 minutes longer, or until the pie shell is golden brown. Transfer the pan to a rack to cool completely.

even flakier pie shell

Substitute 2 tablespoons chilled vegetable shortening, cut into 4 pieces, for 2 tablespoons of the butter. Proceed as directed.

5

a spoonful of comfort

WHEN YOU ARE MAKING a mousse or pudding to take to a dinner party or to give as a thank-you to a neighbor who helped you out, you can certainly put it in a large pretty bowl, but individual servings are nice as well. Depending on the occasion, you can use a variety of containers. For a potluck or other party, spoon the mousse or pudding into pretty ramekins or custard cups, or espresso cups for petite servings. Simply retrieve them at the end of the party or the next day, or make the ramekins or cups part of your gift. The clear colored plastic glasses available at party supply stores are handy disposable containers, while half-pint canning jars, which come with their own lids and can even be stacked, are a homier idea. Put ramekins or other cups on a tray or in a flat basket lined with a festive linen napkin for an attractive presentation, or arrange them in a baking pan so you can transport them easily.

Although these desserts do need to be kept chilled, none of them is so fragile that thirty minutes or so out of the refrigerator will do any harm. They should, of course, be refrigerated once they reach their destination.

lemon mousse

Serves 6 to 8

Folding whipped cream into an intensely flavored lemon custard base creates an easy, sophisticated mousse that you can adapt to your own taste by varying the amount of cream you add. Use the full 3 cups for a lighter, creamier version, 2 to 2½ cups for a more pronounced lemon flavor and a slightly denser consistency (the yield will vary depending on the amount of cream you use). The custard base keeps extremely well, so you can make it days ahead and then finish the mousse whenever you wish.

6 tablespoons unsalted butter, cut into chunks
4 large egg yolks
¾ cup sugar
1½ tablespoons grated lemon zest
¾ cup fresh lemon juice (from 4 large lemons)

2 to 3 cups heavy cream
3 to 4½ tablespoons sugar

1. Melt the butter in a large saucepan (preferably not aluminum, which could react with the lemon juice) over medium heat. Remove the pan from the heat and set it aside.

2. In a medium bowl, beat the egg yolks and sugar with an electric mixer on medium speed until thick and pale, about 2 minutes. On low speed, beat in the lemon zest and juice until thoroughly blended. Transfer the mixture to the saucepan of butter and cook over low to medium-low heat, stirring constantly with a wooden spoon or a heatproof spatula, until the filling is very thick and coats the back of the spoon, 7 to 10 minutes; do not let the custard boil.

3. Strain the custard through a sieve (to remove the lemon zest) into a small bowl and let cool. Cover and refrigerate it until cold, at least 2 hours. *(The custard can be made up to 5 days ahead.)*

4. Combine the cream and sugar (use 1½ tablespoons sugar for each cup of cream) in a large bowl and beat until the cream just holds firm peaks. Using a rubber spatula, gently but thoroughly fold the custard into the cream.

5. Transfer the mousse to a serving bowl or individual serving dishes and refrigerate for at least 1 hour. *(The mousse can be refrigerated, tightly covered, for up to 1 day.)*

instant chocolate mousse

Serves 6

Well, not quite instant, but it really takes just a few minutes to make. Vary the flavoring as you like: Grand Marnier is good in place of the Kahlúa. Lighter when just made, the mousse becomes firmer as it chills—the choice is yours. It's rich, so serve it in small portions.

> *8 ounces bittersweet or semisweet chocolate, finely chopped*
> *1½ cups heavy cream*
> *1½ to 2 tablespoons Kahlúa or 1½ teaspoons pure vanilla extract*

1. Combine the chocolate and ¼ cup of the cream in a small heavy saucepan and heat over very low heat, stirring frequently, until the chocolate is melted and smooth. Transfer to a large bowl and let cool until just barely warm to the touch.

2. Combine the remaining 1¼ cups cream and the Kahlúa in a medium bowl and beat with an electric mixer until the cream just holds soft peaks (do not overbeat, or the mousse may be grainy). Add the cream to the chocolate mixture and, working quickly, fold the chocolate into the cream with a rubber spatula just until incorporated.

3. Transfer the mousse to a serving bowl or individual serving dishes and refrigerate for at least 1 hour. *(The mousse can be refrigerated, tightly covered, for up to 1 day.)*

chocolate-chunk chocolate mousse

For a contrast in textures, add chocolate chunks to the mousse. Fold 2 ounces bittersweet or semisweet chocolate, coarsely chopped, into the mousse as soon as the chocolate mixture is incorporated.

silky secret-ingredient chocolate mousse

Mascarpone, the rich creamy Italian cheese (available in many supermarkets), adds richness and a satiny texture to the mousse, yet its slightly tangy flavor is almost undetectable. Add 1 cup mascarpone to the cream and Kahlúa and whisk gently until smooth. Beat until the mixture just holds soft peaks and proceed as directed. (Serves 6 to 8)

really chocolate chocolate pudding

Serves 6

Far better than anything you remember from childhood, this deep chocolate pudding is suave enough to serve at a dinner party (spoon it into martini glasses for an elegant touch). Or make it for kids (of any age) when they need a bit of old-fashioned comfort. The pudding is best made at least six hours, or even a day, ahead to allow the flavors to mellow and deepen. (You can also use this as the filling for chocolate cream pie; see the variation.)

2 cups whole milk
⅔ cup heavy cream
1 cup sugar
3 tablespoons cornstarch
4 large egg yolks
Pinch of salt
8 ounces bittersweet chocolate, finely chopped
1½ teaspoons pure vanilla extract

1. Combine 1¾ cups plus 2 tablespoons of the milk, the cream, and sugar in a large heavy saucepan and bring to a boil over medium-low heat, stirring occasionally to dissolve the sugar.
2. Meanwhile, whisk together the cornstarch and the remaining 2 tablespoons milk in a medium bowl until smooth. Add the egg yolks and salt and whisk until smooth.
3. Whisking constantly, gradually add about half of the hot milk mixture to the yolks, then return the mixture to the saucepan and cook over low heat, stirring constantly with a heatproof rubber spatula or a wooden spoon, until the mixture comes to a boil. Boil, stirring constantly, for 1 minute (the mixture will thicken), then remove the pan from the heat and add the chocolate. Stir gently until the chocolate is melted and the pudding is smooth. Stir in the vanilla.
4. Transfer the mousse to a serving bowl or individual serving dishes and let cool to room temperature. Refrigerate, covered, for at least 6 hours or, preferably, overnight.

chocolate cream pie

Scrape the cooled pudding into a prebaked Flaky Pie Shell (page 98). Refrigerate for at least 6 hours and, if you wish, garnish with whipped cream and chocolate curls.

strawberries and cream with brown sugar sauce

Serves 6

Take three ingredients, layer them together in minutes, put them in the refrigerator for a few hours while the brown sugar melts into a sauce, and you've got the simplest, freshest dessert to take to a friend's dinner party. I used to make this with sour cream, but crème fraîche—increasingly available in supermarkets and in any gourmet market—updates it and gives it a richer, more mellow flavor. Prepare this in a glass bowl to show off its distinctive layers, then scoop out individual servings of berries, cream, and sauce.

> *2 pints fresh strawberries, rinsed, dried, hulled, and quartered*
> *12 ounces crème fraîche*
> *5 to 6 tablespoons packed dark brown sugar*

1. Put the strawberries in a large glass bowl. Spread the crème fraîche gently over the berries in a thin, even layer. Sprinkle the brown sugar evenly over the cream, breaking up any lumps with your fingers.

2. Cover the berries and refrigerate for at least 3 hours. *(The dessert can be prepared up to 8 hours ahead.)*

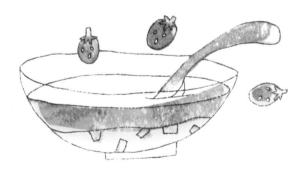

6

a few special little treats

BE IMAGINATIVE when you wrap or package these "better than store-bought" confections and sauces for your favorite people. Look for pretty tins and boxes at gift shops. Or fill a mug with Candied Orange Peel (page 108) and wrap it in colored cellophane. A jar each of The Best Hot Fudge Sauce (page 114) and Caramel Sauce (page 115) snuggled in a small basket will delight an elderly neighbor who loves ice cream, and a colorful party bag stuffed with Totally Unlike Store-Bought Caramels (page 110) or Candied Pecans (page 112) and tied with a satin ribbon says thank you to a coworker who was especially helpful during a difficult project.

candied orange peel

Makes about 2½ cups

Candied orange peel is surprisingly easy to make, though it does require some time in the kitchen as you wait for the strips of peel to cook to the proper softness in the sugar syrup (just about the right amount of time, in fact, to wrap the Totally Unlike Store-Bought Caramels, page 110, you've made for someone else). A delectable treat on its own, perhaps with after-dinner coffee, the candied peel makes a lovely garnish, left whole or chopped or minced, for many desserts.

3 large navel oranges, scrubbed
3 tablespoons light corn syrup
1 cup sugar, plus about ¾ cup for coating
1 cup water

1. Using a serrated knife or other sharp knife, cut a thin slice off the top and bottom of each orange to expose the flesh. Score the peel of each orange into quarters, cutting through the white pith, and pull the quarters of peel off the orange. Using a sharp spoon, scrape off any stringy membranes from the inside of the peel (do not scrape off the white pith). Cut each quarter crosswise into ¼-inch-wide strips.

2. Put the orange peel in a large heavy saucepan, add cold water to cover, and bring to a boil; drain. Repeat two more times (blanching the peel removes the bitterness). Return the orange peel to the saucepan, add cold water to cover by about 1 inch, and bring to a boil. Reduce the heat and simmer gently, stirring occasionally, until the peel is tender when pierced with a knife, about 15 minutes; drain and set aside.

3. Set a large wire rack, preferably a mesh one, over a baking sheet; set aside. Combine the corn syrup, sugar, and water in the same saucepan and bring to a boil, stirring to dissolve the sugar. Wash down the sides of the pan with a wet pastry brush to remove any sugar crystals (which could cause the syrup to crystallize) and add the orange peel. Bring to a simmer, reduce the heat, and simmer gently, stirring once or twice with a clean spoon, until the peel is translucent and very tender and the syrup has reduced to a few spoonfuls, 30 to 40 minutes. (Do not allow the syrup to reduce to less than this, or the bottom of the pan will become too hot and will crystallize the sugar.)

4. Using a slotted spoon or a fork, transfer the peel to the wire rack to drain; be sure to separate all the strips of peel. Let cool.

5. Put the sugar for coating in a small bowl and toss the orange peel a few strips at a time in the sugar, coating them thoroughly, then transfer the peel to a clean wire rack. Let stand until dry, at least 4 hours. *(Once the orange peel is thoroughly dry, it can be stored in an airtight tin at room temperature for up to 1 week.)*

candied lemon peel

Substitute 6 lemons for the oranges. Proceed as directed.

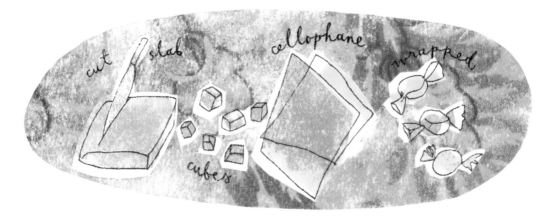

totally unlike store-bought caramels

Makes 100 caramels

Rich and chewy, but not too chewy, homemade caramels are nothing like the grocery store variety. Although making them does take some time, there is very little real work involved. You will need a candy thermometer, but even if this is the only recipe you ever use it for, you will find the minimal investment more than worth it. I have one friend who calls me every year at Christmastime to ask for this recipe, which she can never find when she needs it. Keep in mind that caramel does not like humidity—it might not set up—so make these candies on a dry day.

These are two-bite-size caramels, but you can cut them into slightly smaller bites if you prefer. For a fancy touch, wrap the caramels in colored or clear cellophane, which is sold with the wrapping paper at party shops. Waxed paper also works well, and the homier look has its own appeal.

> *2 cups sugar*
> *2 cups heavy cream*
> *1¾ cups light corn syrup*
> *½ pound (2 sticks) unsalted butter, cut into chunks*
> *Pinch of salt*
> *1½ teaspoons pure vanilla extract*

1. Lightly butter the bottom and sides of a 9-by-13-inch baking pan (this will anchor the foil), then line the pan with foil, pressing the foil smoothly over the bottom and up the sides. Lightly butter the foil (including the sides).

2. Butter the sides of a large heavy pot. Add the sugar, 1 cup of the cream, the corn syrup, butter, and salt and cook over medium heat, stirring with a wooden spoon, until the butter has melted and the sugar has completely dissolved. Wash down the sides of the pot with a wet pastry brush to remove any sugar crystals (which could cause the caramel to crystallize). Bring the mixture to a boil, then wash down the sides of the pot again and attach a candy thermometer to the pot. Cook at a moderate boil, without stirring, until the mixture reaches 242°F, 25 to 30 minutes.

3. Add the remaining 1 cup cream very slowly, so the mixture remains at a boil, and stir gently with a clean wooden spoon. Boil, without stirring, until the mixture reaches 246°F, about 20 minutes longer.

4. Remove the pot from the heat, add the vanilla, and stir just to blend. Pour the caramel into the prepared baking pan; do not be tempted to scrape the caramel from the bottom of the pot, as the caramel may crystallize (but scrape it into a heatproof bowl, if you like, to cool for a cook's nibble). Set the baking pan on a rack to cool completely, then cover the pan with plastic wrap and let stand at room temperature for at least 4 hours, or overnight, to mellow the flavors.

5. Turn the caramel slab out onto a cutting board and peel off the foil. Using a sharp heavy knife, cut the slab crosswise into 10 strips, then cut each strip into 10 caramels. Wrap each caramel in cellophane or waxed paper. *(The caramels can be stored in an airtight container at room temperature for up to 1 week; they can be refrigerated for up to 2 weeks or frozen for up to 1 month.)*

candied pecans

Makes about 2 cups

A great sweet snack on their own, candied pecans make an unusual garnish for a mousse, pudding, or other dessert. You can sweeten other nuts as well—hazelnuts and almonds are both good choices.

> ¾ cup sugar
>
> ¼ cup water
>
> 1½ cups (about 6 ounces) pecan halves

1. Lightly grease a baking sheet.

2. Combine the sugar and water in a large heavy saucepan and bring to a boil over medium-high heat, stirring until the sugar dissolves. Wash down the sides of the pan with a wet pastry brush to remove any sugar crystals (which could cause the caramel to crystallize). Boil, without stirring, until the caramel is a golden amber color, 5 to 8 minutes; once the caramel starts to darken in color, swirl the pan occasionally so the caramel cooks evenly. Remove the pan from the heat and immediately add the pecans, stirring with a wooden spoon until the nuts are well coated. Working quickly, scrape the mixture out onto the greased baking sheet, using two wooden spoons or spatulas to spread out the nuts as much as possible and separate any big clusters of nuts. Let cool completely.

3. Break up any remaining clusters of nuts and transfer to an airtight container. (*The nuts can be stored at room temperature for up to 1 week.*)

truffle squares

Makes 36 large or 64 small truffles

These sleek, streamlined truffles are made by chilling a chocolate cream mixture, then cutting it into squares rather than rolling the ganache between your palms into balls—the traditional but messy procedure. To customize your truffles, substitute Kahlúa or another liqueur for the Grand Marnier; and you might dust half of the truffles with cocoa and half with confectioners' sugar. Pack them, layered between sheets of waxed paper, in a little tin for that special chocolate lover.

> *12 ounces bittersweet chocolate, coarsely chopped*
> *¾ cup heavy cream*
> *1½ tablespoons Grand Marnier or 1½ teaspoons pure vanilla extract*
> *About ⅓ cup unsweetened cocoa powder (see page 12), sifted*

1. Line an 8-inch square baking pan with foil, letting the foil extend over two opposite sides of the pan.

2. Put the chocolate in a food processor and process until finely chopped. Bring the cream to a boil in a small saucepan. With the machine running, add the cream to the processor and process just until the chocolate is completely melted, stopping once or twice to scrape down the sides of the bowl. Add the Grand Marnier and process just to blend.

3. Pour the mixture into the prepared pan, spread it evenly with a rubber spatula, and let cool. Cover tightly and place in the freezer until firm, 3 to 4 hours.

4. Use the foil to lift the truffle slab out of the pan; invert the slab onto a cutting board and carefully peel off the foil. You may find it's easiest to cut the chocolate with a warm knife: Dip a sharp heavy knife in hot water, then wipe it thoroughly dry and cut the truffles into 36 or 64 squares, rewarming the knife as necessary. If the truffle mixture becomes too soft, return it briefly to the freezer to firm. Arrange the truffles in a single layer on a large plate or platter and refrigerate, uncovered, for 1 hour.

5. Put the cocoa powder in a small shallow bowl. Toss the truffles a few at a time in the cocoa to coat, then shake them gently in a sieve to remove excess cocoa; transfer to another plate. Refrigerate the truffles for 1 hour. If necessary, toss them again in cocoa to coat; return them to the refrigerator. *(The truffles can be stored in the refrigerator for up to 3 days.)*

the best hot fudge sauce

Makes about 1¼ cups

Thick and fudgy, with undertones of caramel, this sauce is the ultimate sundae sauce. When I somewhat sheepishly admitted to eating it straight out of the jar, friends confided that they do the same.

> ½ cup heavy cream
> 4 tablespoons unsalted butter, cut into 4 pieces
> ½ cup packed light brown sugar
> Scant ¼ cup granulated sugar
> Pinch of salt
> ½ cup unsweetened cocoa powder (see page 12)
> ½ teaspoon pure vanilla extract

1. In a medium heavy saucepan, combine the cream, butter, both sugars, and salt and bring to a simmer over medium heat, stirring to dissolve the sugar. Reduce the heat to medium low and simmer, stirring occasionally, for 2 minutes. Reduce the heat to low and add the cocoa powder, whisking until smooth.

2. Transfer the sauce to a bowl and stir in the vanilla. Serve hot or warm. *(The sauce can be refrigerated for up to 3 days. Reheat in a double boiler over low heat, stirring frequently, or in the microwave.)*

caramel sauce

Makes about 1½ cups

Spoon this sauce over ice cream (along with The Best Hot Fudge Sauce, page 114, for a super sundae or drizzle a little over sliced ripe peaches or poached pears. For a thinner sauce, increase the cream to 1½ cups; for an even thicker sauce, reduce the cream to ¾ cup. For a clear pure caramel sauce, see the variation.

> *1 cup sugar*
> *⅓ cup water*
> *1 cup heavy cream*

1. Combine the sugar and water in a small heavy saucepan and bring to a boil over medium-high heat, stirring occasionally to dissolve the sugar. Wash down the sides of the pan with a wet pastry brush to remove any sugar crystals (which could cause the caramel to crystallize). Boil, without stirring, until the caramel is a golden amber, 5 to 8 minutes; once the caramel starts to darken in color, swirl the pan occasionally so the caramel cooks evenly.

2. Immediately remove the pan from the heat and, standing back, slowly add the cream (the mixture will bubble up). Return the pan to low heat and cook, stirring with a wooden spoon, until any lumps of caramel have dissolved and the sauce is smooth. Remove the pan from the heat and serve the sauce warm or at room temperature. *(The sauce can be refrigerated for up to 5 days; rewarm over low heat, stirring occasionally.)*

clear caramel sauce

Omit the cream and add ½ cup water to the caramel in step 2. Cook the caramel over low heat, stirring occasionally, until it is completely smooth. For a thicker sauce, bring to a boil and cook, stirring occasionally, until it is slightly syrupy. (Makes about 1 cup)

EPILOGUE

*I fed Parsley her biscuits for elderly cats,
and she drowsed on the shelf above the radiator. Parsley was sixteen,
which I tried my best to ignore. She held my heart in her killer
tawny paw and, as far as I was concerned, she must live forever.*

—ELIZABETH BUCHAN, Revenge of the Middle-Aged Woman

When she was sixteen, Remy, "the Million-Dollar Miracle Cat," finally ran out of miracles. She was fat and happy until almost the very end, but things suddenly went wrong, and she died in September 2003, with Dr. Rocha and me at her side. The night before she went into the hospital for what would be the last time, I knew I wouldn't be able to sleep, so I baked two batches of Brown Sugar Shortbread at midnight. I had a pound of butter in the freezer, and measuring the sugar and flour, creaming the butter, and patting the dough into the pan were somehow soothing, at least a little.

Knowing my belief that chocolate helps in even the most dire circumstances, many people sent me chocolate after Remy died (the vet's office sent yellow roses). My good "food friends" Ann and Debbie sent a three-pound slab of Scharffen Berger special bittersweet 70% chocolate, with the wish and idea that it might inspire a special dessert in Remy's honor. A month or so later, I did use it to perfect the Very Special Fudgy Brownies (though I know Remy would have preferred foie gras and caviar). In the six months after Remy died, I finished this book; it helped to be baking desserts for friends and others while always having some sort of comforting treat around.

Life goes on, and now there's another cat sitting on my desk looking at the birds in the tree outside my window. Like Remy, Roxy is a rescued cat. A kindhearted couple with the Big Apple Circus found her, a tiny, starving kitten, on a cold rainy day in Atlanta, Georgia, and brought her north with them. When they decided they couldn't keep her, they contacted a pet rescue group that posted her story on the Internet. She's a funny, feisty girl—and she did her best to help me with the book, monitoring each page as it came out of my printer (and sticking in her paw if it seemed necessary). These days, I'm taking brownies to the vet whenever Roxy needs a checkup.

ACKNOWLEDGMENTS

There are many really important people I would like to thank:

Ann Bramson, who believed in this idea long before it became a book; Deborah Weiss Geline, for her thoughtful suggestions, sensitive editing, and longtime support; Pamela Cannon, for her enthusiasm and dedication to the book; Vivian Ghazarian, for her engaging design; and Amy Corley, Danielle Costa, Nancy Murray, Nick Caruso, Ellice Goldstein, and Barbara Peragine.

Mariko Jesse, for her charming and whimsical illustrations.

Mickey Choate, my great agent—it is really no exaggeration to say that without him, this book would never have happened.

Dr. Tim Rocha, for his care of Remy—and his love of desserts. And all the other caretakers and dessert tasters at Manhattan Vet.

My loyal friends, who helped me in so many ways throughout the writing of *Sweet Gratitude*—especially Tish Boyle, Mary Goodbody, and Lori Longbotham, for culinary consultations; and Sharon Bowers and Catherine Jones, for recipe testing. And, of course, my family.

INDEX

a

almonds:

in easy raspberry linzer squares, 56–57

in raspberry linzer hearts, 38–39

amazing toffee thins, 30–31

apple and brown butter crostata, 96–97

b

baby scones with dried cherries or blueberries, 45

bars, *see* brownies and bars

berry:

filling, 87

tartlets with sweet mascarpone, 84

see also specific berries

best hot fudge sauce, 114

blackberries, in mascarpone filling, 84

black pepper, in spicy English gingersnaps, 32–33

blueberry(ies):

baby scones with, 45

in berry filling, 87

-lemon upside-down cake, 73

in mascarpone filling, 84

-raspberry tart, 87

brown butter:

and apple crostata, 96–97

filling, 96–97

brownies and bars, 47–57

caramel-topped turtle, 50–51

ganache-filled brown sugar, 54–55

inside-out brown sugar bars, 55

lemon coconut, 52

refined chocolate coconut, 52

shipping of, 19–20

storing and freezing of, 18–19

very special fudgy, 48–49

wrapping of, 20–21

see also squares

brown sugar:

in amazing toffee thins, 30–31

bars, ganache-filled, 54–55

bars, inside-out, 55

in best hot fudge sauce, 114

in blueberry-lemon upside-down cake, 73

in caramel-topped turtle brownies, 50–51

in cherry-chocolate chip upside-down cake, 73

in chocolate espresso sandwich cookies, 36–37

in chunky chocolate chip cookies, 25

cut-out cookies, 40–41

in devil's food cupcakes, 61–62

in ginger-peach upside-down cake, 72–73

sauce, strawberries and cream with, 105

shortbread, 42

slice-and-bake cookies, 41

in spicy English gingersnaps, 32–33

tips on, 16

in two-ginger gingerbread, 74–75

in very special fudgy brownies, 48–49

Buchan, Elizabeth, 116

little lemon loaves, 78–79

Lorna Doones, 52

m

macaroons:

    chocolate chip coconut, 35

    melt-in-your-mouth coconut, 34–35

marionberries, in mascarpone filling, 84

mascarpone:

    filling, 84

    in silky secret-ingredient chocolate mousse, 103

    sweet, berry tartlets with, 84

Matthew's birthday cake, 63

Medaglia d'Oro, 36, 93

melt-in-your-mouth coconut macaroons, 34–35

mocha:

    filling, 93

    silk pie, 93

molasses:

    dark, in spicy English gingersnaps, 32–33

    in two-ginger gingerbread, 74–75

mousse, 101

    chocolate-chunk chocolate, 103

    instant chocolate, 103

    lemon, 102

    silky sweet secret-ingredient chocolate, 103

    see also pudding

n

Nestlé, 12

o

old-fashioned spice cake with cream cheese
    frosting, 70–71

orange(s):

    cupcakes with orange cream cheese frosting, 64–65

    juice, in cranberry-cherry filling, 92

    peel, candied, 108–9

    tips on, 17

p

peach:

    -ginger topping, 72

    -ginger upside-down cake, 72–73

peanut butter:

    filling, 94–95

    pie, whipped cream, 95

    pie with a chocolate cookie crust, 94–95

peanut butter cookies:

    chocolate chip–, 27

    with crunch, 26–27

    jumbo, 27

pecans:

    candied, 112

    halves, in caramel topping, 51

    in refined chocolate coconut bars, 52

peels:

    candied lemon, 109

    candied orange, 108–9

petticoat tails, ginger-ginger, 43

pies, 81–82, 92–99

    chocolate cream, 104

    cranberry and dried cherry, 92

    mocha silk, 93

    peanut butter, with a chocolate cookie crust, 94–95

    storing and freezing of, 18–19

    whipped cream peanut butter, 95